COLORADO
MOUNTAIN CLUB
PACK GUIDE

THE BEST
Moab
and Arches
National Park
HIKES

D1594216

The Colorado Mountain Club Press
Golden, Colorado

The Best Moab and Arches National Park Hikes
© 2015 by The Colorado Mountain Club

PUBLISHED BY

The Colorado Mountain Club Press
710 Tenth Street, Suite 200, Golden, Colorado 80401
303-996-2743   e-mail: cmcpress@cmc.org

Founded in 1912, The Colorado Mountain Club is the largest outdoor recreation, education, and conservation organization in the Rocky Mountains. Look for our books at your local bookstore or outdoor retailer or online at www.cmc.org/store.

Rod Martinez: author, photographer
John Gascoyne: series editor
Eduard B. Avis: copy editor
Erika K. Arroyo: design, composition, and production
Sarah Gorecki: publisher

CONTACTING THE PUBLISHER
We would appreciate it if readers would alert us to any errors or outdated information by contacting us at the address above.

DISTRIBUTED TO THE BOOK TRADE BY
The Mountaineers Books, 1001 SW Klickitat Way, Suite 201, Seattle, WA 98134, 800-553-4453, www.mountaineersbooks.org

TOPOGRAPHIC MAPS are copyright 2009 and were created using National Geographic TOPO! Outdoor Recreation software (www.natgeomaps.com; 800-962-1643).

COVER PHOTO: Delicate Arch in Arches National Park, Utah.
Photo by Rod Martinez

We gratefully acknowledge the financial support of the people of Colorado through the Scientific and Cultural Facilities District of greater Denver for our publishing activities.

WARNING: Although there has been an effort to make the trail descriptions in this book as accurate as possible, some discrepancies may exist between the text and the trails in the field. Hiking in mountainous areas—and canyons and deserts as well—is a high-risk activity. This guidebook is not a substitute for your experience and common sense. The users of this guidebook assume full responsibility for their own safety. Weather, terrain conditions, and individual abilities must be considered before undertaking any of the hikes in this guide.

First Edition

ISBN 978-1-937052-14-0
Ebook ISBN 978-1-937052-20-1

Printed in Korea

The Best Moab and Arches National Park Hikes pack guide is dedicated to two great friends, Jim and Darleen Nelson. Jim and Darleen have been residents of Moab at least as long as I have been hiking in the Moab area. Jim has led my long-time friend and hiking partner Jerry and me on many excursions. At times we had no idea where we were going, but we always found rarely-seen rock art or a new arch or canyon to explore.

Jim's wife, Darleen, always made Jerry and me welcome at her dinner table. Darleen is also known as the "pie lady." I never visited Moab without enjoying a delectable piece of a variety of pies. Thanks, Jim and Darleen, for making Moab feel like a second home.

As always, this pack guide is also dedicated to my wife, Sue, as well as to my marvelous daughter-in-law, Stephanie, my two sons, John and Chris, and my three beautiful granddaughters, Brittany, Nichole, and Samantha.

I would like to recognize the efforts of all the state, national park, and Bureau of Land Management rangers. Thanks and gratitude must also be given to all the volunteers at all state and national parks and monuments. These dedicated people make our visits to all public lands safe and enjoyable, while helping to preserve their natural beauty.

Horseshoe Shelter pictographs in Horseshoe Canyon.

PHOTO BY ROD MARTINEZ

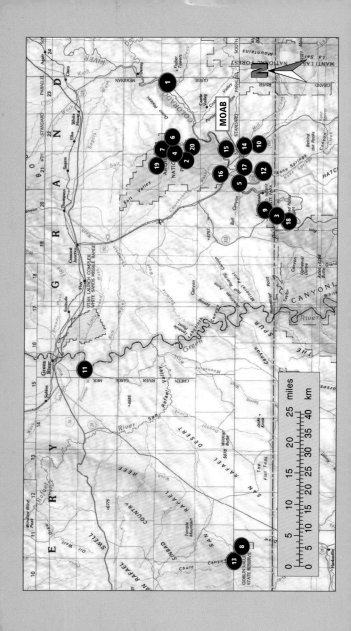

CONTENTS

The Birthing Scene petroglyph along Kane Creek Road.

ACKNOWLEDGMENTS

It is an honor to be the author of CMC Press's first pack guide for the State of Utah. For me, hiking, photographing, and having my efforts published are a dream come true. Thanks to John Gascoyne for again being a mentor and contributing his knowledge in making this pack guide the success that it's certain to become. Besides that, John is a lot of fun to just chat with.

To my publisher, Sarah Gorecki, tremendous thanks for the foresight and support in having this pack guide published. Thanks also to Sarah for having faith and trust in me to complete all the hikes for her maiden voyage in publishing a pack guide for CMC. I also thank Sarah for stepping beyond the boundaries of Colorado and embracing Utah as a new endeavor for CMC Press. This is a great team that will put forth other exciting and helpful pack guides.

—*ROD MARTINEZ*

Orange—an uncommon color for a prickly pear cactus bloom.

PHOTO BY ROD MARTINEZ

FOREWORD

The 20 hiking trails in this pack guide range in location from one of the most popular national parks in Utah—Arches National Park—to one of the more remote areas in Utah—Horseshoe Canyon. This book will guide you to the world famous Delicate Arch and to Landscape Arch—one of the world's largest natural rock spans. It also will take you to Dead Horse Point State Park, where you can peer 2,000 feet down to the Colorado River, and to trails in canyons carved by eons of water coursing through sandstone rock. Take plenty of water on any moderate to difficult hike. Stay hydrated as you hike the hot arid trails described in this pack guide. A good practice is to keep extra water in your vehicle—you can drink some before you leave and know that there will be some waiting for you when you return.

RATINGS

What distinguishes the difficulty rating of the hikes? Each hiker will see differences in what is termed easy, moderate, and difficult. On occasion, a particularly challenging hike will be described as difficult–strenuous. In the world of rock climbers, the most difficult part of a climb, even a short stretch, determines the rating of the entire climb. Likewise in this book, the most challenging part of any hike will determine how we rate it.

Among elements in establishing the ratings are:

Elevation gain. A 1,000-foot gain in elevation for a round-trip hike of 3 to 4 miles may be as difficult, or as strenuous, as a hike gaining 1,200 feet in a 6- to 8-mile round-trip.

Round-trip distance. Normally, an 8- to 10-mile hike is more difficult or strenuous than one of 4 to 6 miles.

Trail characteristics. Is the trail well marked, or do you need to search for continuation of the trail? Are boulder hopping or scree slopes involved? Are there creek/stream crossings, and are they easy or is wading involved? As the difficult elements add up or increase in severity, so will the difficulty rating.

WEATHER

Be aware of and prepared for changes in the weather. If it looks like rain, consider doing the hike another day. An early start will decrease the odds of encountering afternoon thunderstorms. If the weather begins to deteriorate while you are hiking, be cautious and consider turning around. All the hikes in this pack guide can be hiked any season of the year. Late spring to early fall is the hottest time of year in Moab and Arches National Park. Temperatures may exceed 100 degrees in the afternoon during summer. Leave early in the morning when it is cooler, but, as noted, always take plenty of water. Please read the side note on the dangers and potential of flash flooding in canyons.

ROUND-TRIP TIME

The time it takes to complete a hike depends on the physical ability of the hikers, the prevailing weather, and the purpose of the hike. The hikes described in this pack guide might be among the first hikes for some readers and, consequently, it might take them longer to get acclimated to the altitude and tone up muscles not recently exercised. Other hikers might be better acclimated and in great shape. The time it takes them to complete these hikes may be considerably shorter.

I happen to be a slow hiker, because I pause frequently to catch my breath and enjoy the scenery. I also stop to take photographs—lots of them. I am not a point-and-shoot photographer—I work at getting the best possible photo (see photography tips on page 22 of this pack guide), so it can take more time to capture the image I am seeking. The times listed in this pack guide are based on average hikers who want to enjoy their hike. For those who hike more quickly for outdoor exercise, the times probably will be shorter. Again, I recommend you start early to avoid afternoon storms, and begin your return trip in time to make it back to the trailhead before it becomes dark.

SAFETY

The Ten Essentials Systems, on pages 18-21 of this pack guide, are the Colorado Mountain Club's "systems" to promote safety awareness and to give you a list of safety items to carry at all times when hiking. Please take the time to read, study, and absorb all the Ten Essentials.

Here are some additional safety measures to consider and make habits of:

- Tell someone where you plan to go and when you plan to return. Be specific and stay on the trail. Tell that person to contact authorities in the area you are hiking if she or he does not hear from you by an appointed time.
- Sign in at the trail register. Sign out when you return.
- Consider carrying an emergency locater device. In life-threatening circumstances, it can notify emergency personnel where you are and that you need their help. Keep it readily accessible so you can reach it when necessary. When not hiking, keep it in your vehicle— just in case. There are several available, with various useful features, at outdoor equipment retailers.

LEAVE NO TRACE

We owe it to present and future generations to care for the wild places. If you pack it in, pack it out—leave only footprints:

- Plan ahead and prepare for the cleanest possible adventure.
- Stay on the trail and don't shortcut the switchbacks; camp on durable surfaces, such as rock or sand. Please read the side note on "The Soil is Alive" so you can avoid damaging the delicate soil in the desert areas you will be hiking in. If more than one person needs to go

off trail, spread out so you don't start destructive new "social" trails.

- Dispose of all waste properly, including that deposited by your dog. "Pack it in, pack it out."
- Leave what you find and don't pick it up—look at it, take a photo, leave it for the next person.
- Minimize campfire impacts—think small and keep the fuel within the fire circle. Unless it is a permanent fire pit, destroy all traces of your fire before leaving your campsite. Forest fires have started from small camp fires or their smoldering embers; be extremely cautious in this regard. The best practice is to completely soak down your fire site.
- Respect wildlife—although there are deer, pronghorn antelope, and bighorn sheep in the area, they are rarely seen. Don't feed animals anything and don't intrude on their feeding and breeding areas.
- Be considerate of animals and other humans on the trail—don't play your radio or make other unnecessary noise. Part of the lure of the outdoors is the healing sound of the wind through the trees, or the murmur of a stream.

—*Rod Martinez*

A distant view of Corona Arch reveals how it is abutted to the rock cliff.
PHOTO BY ROD MARTINEZ

Introduction

Words cannot adequately describe the Moab area and Arches National Park. The scenery is incredible, the outdoor recreational opportunities are endless, and the City of Moab is constantly active. Moab is the hub of southeast Utah and Arches National Park and Canyonlands National Park are the main attractions of the area. Moab by itself is an attraction that is like no other in the State of Utah.

THE AREA: Hiking and photography are two of my life's passions. The Moab area and Arches National Park allow me to fully enjoy these important pursuits in Red Rock Country. If you wanted to hike every trail in the Moab area and Arches you could spend many weeks in pursuit of that goal.

> ### Caveat—on maps and map scales
>
> In producing this pack guide, we have endeavored to provide the most accurate information possible. This striving for accuracy includes the map segments that follow each trail description. Many of the trails indicated by the red lines, however, include contours, ups and downs, and switchbacks that cannot be depicted on a small map. Thus, with some maps, you may find what looks like a variance between the stated length of the trail and the length of the trail when compared to the scale indicator.
>
> For every trail described in this guide, we list relevant, larger-scale maps of the area you will be hiking in—such as Trails Illustrated and USGS maps. It is always a good practice to secure these larger maps, study them, and understand where the smaller map from the guide fits within the larger map. The best practice is to carry both maps on your hike.

Arches National Park is renowned for having 2,000-plus arches within the park boundary. This is the largest concentration of natural stone arches in the world. An arch is defined as a hole in the rock that must have an opening at least three feet long in any direction. A natural bridge is formed by running water and spans a former or present waterway. Morning Glory Natural Bridge in Negro Bill Canyon is the sixth largest stone bridge in the world. Almost every hike in Arches National Park will take you to or near an arch.

HIKING: The hikes in Arches National Park range from a 10-minute walk around Balanced Rock to a 5-hour, 7.2-mile hike of the Primitive Loop in the Devils Garden area. Trails in the Moab area take you to other impressive arches or into canyons that have running water all year round. Trails in Dead Horse Point State Park allow the hiker to stand on the edge of a canyon and peer 2,000 feet below to the Colorado River.

Canyonlands National Park is 337,570 acres in size. The Green River and Colorado River divide the park into four districts: Island in the Sky, The Needles, The Maze, and the rivers themselves. It would take a long time to hike all the trails in Canyonlands. The hikes and trails of Canyonlands National Park will be described in a future pack guide, except for the trail into Horseshoe Canyon, which is detailed in this pack guide. Horseshoe Canyon is a recent addition to the Maze District, but is readily accessible from Moab. Horseshoe Canyon contains what is generally considered the most significant rock art in North America.

SO MUCH TO DO: The hikes and trails in this pack guide are not limited to the immediate Moab area: Within 90 miles, there are great hikes in the San Rafael Swell. A few different hikes are located near Goblin Valley State Park; this five-square-

> **Water no-no's**
>
> As you hike trails in this and other pack guides, some of them will take you by, and over, creeks and streams. Do not drink the water from these creeks and streams without filtering or otherwise treating it. The water, while tempting and offering refreshment, may contain the parasite known as giardia. Individuals become infected by ingesting or coming into contact with contaminated food, soil, or water. The symptoms of giardia, which may begin to appear two days after infection, include violent diarrhea, excess gas, stomach or abdominal cramps, upset stomach, and nausea. This serious inconvenience can last for a good number of days and medical treatment is advisable.

mile state park has thousands of hoodoos and hoodoo rocks, locally referred to as goblins. The trail into Little Wild Horse Canyon will take you into a slot canyon. Slot canyons are formed by the wear of water rushing through rock and are especially prevalent in the sandstone found in Utah. A slot canyon may be only a few feet wide but the canyon itself will be significantly deeper—a work of art sculpted in many different forms and patterns as the water erodes the rock.

CLIMBING: If you enjoy rock climbing, the Moab area offers many different challenges. The big walls around Moab, including along Potash Road and the Colorado Riverway, offer every conceivable challenge. The Fisher Towers have their own challenges due to the composition of the rock; years ago one husband and wife climbing/photographing team described them as "...crumbly rock sandwiched between layers of kitty litter." The Titan is over 900 feet tall and was first successfully climbed in 1962. The Titan is the largest of the Fisher Towers and the largest free-standing tower in the United States.

Rock climbing in Arches and Canyonlands National Parks is permitted, subject to numerous restrictions and regulations. Climbing any arch in Arches National Park is not permitted. Please check with the National Park Service rangers to be sure you are in compliance before attempting any climb in the national parks. Currently, you are allowed to climb and swing via rope from the arches on Bureau of Land Management land, as I discuss in the Corona Arch Trail hike in this pack guide. Be aware that this is a highly dangerous, sometimes deadly, enterprise, so please do not attempt to swing from any of the arches on any sort of rope.

WATER SPORTS: Kayaking and rafting are great outdoor activities in the area—from late spring through mid-fall. A safe and smooth whitewater raft trip on the section of the Colorado River by Fisher Towers is family oriented. A wilder and more intense raft trip is available if you launch east of Fisher Towers

The massive Balanced Rock sits on top of a tapered spire.

PHOTO BY ROD MARTINEZ

for a trip through Westwater Canyon or, directly west of Moab, through Cataract Canyon. Canoes and kayaks provide a refreshing way to enjoy the Colorado River on a hot day.

BIKING: Mountain biking is another tremendous draw to the Moab area. It's been said that Moab is home to the greatest mountain biking on the planet and offers a huge variety of trails. Biking opportunities in the Moab area range from the easy, paved trails around Moab, to ones for the more experienced bikers looking for new challenges around the Moab area. Check out www.discovermoab.com to see the many different trails, from the highly technical Slickrock Bike Trail to the expert Rockstacker/Pothole Arch and Jackson Trails. Dead Horse Point State Park has numerous easy to moderate bike trails, including the 9-mile Big Chief Loop Trail. Road biking is available throughout the Moab and Arches National Park area.

FOUR-WHEELING: There are hundreds of miles of four-wheel-drive roads in the area. A novice four-wheeler will have fun and learn how to use their vehicle on easy trails such as Chicken Corners or Secret Spires. Experienced drivers will have their adrenaline pumping on Pritchett Canyon and Golden Spike. Expert drivers will enjoy the challenge of such trails as Metal Masher, Cliff Hanger, Hell's Revenge, and Steel Bender.

EVENTS AND FESTIVALS: In between hikes, take time to enjoy some of the many different annual events Moab offers: the annual April Action Car Show, the Moab Photography Symposium in early May, the annual Moab Arts Festival on Memorial Day weekend, and the Moab Music Festival in September. Perhaps the rowdiest event of the year is the 9-day Easter Jeep Safari. Moab is truly a diverse and spectacular area with a lot of great things to see and do and great places to stay. Moab is also home to the Moab Diner—my favorite place to eat—featuring "Utah's Best Green Chili"!

Entrance fees

Arches National Park

All federal recreational lands passes are issued and accepted at Arches:

- Annual Pass: $80
- Senior Pass: $10 lifetime pass, for U.S. citizens or permanent residents age 62 or over
- Free Annual Pass for U.S. Military: Available to U.S. military members and dependents in the Army, Navy, Air Force, Marines, Coast Guard, and Reserve and National Guard

Dead Horse Point State Park

- Day-use fee: $10 per vehicle for up to eight passengers; $5 for Utah seniors 62 and older

NOTE: *These fees reflect prices as of fall 2014, the writing of the first edition of this pack guide. Prices, of course, are subject to change so please contact the park if there is any question.*

SPECIAL SAFETY NOTE

When hiking the canyons around Moab, in particular the slot canyons, be aware of the weather. Rain will run off the slick-rock and follow a canyon to the lower areas. Slot canyons—the narrowest rock apertures—are the most vulnerable, but all canyons can experience flash flooding after a rain. The water will be fast and deep—be aware of the weather and avoid slot canyons if rain is anywhere close to where you are, or even if you are aware of rainfall quite some distance away.

In August 1997, 11 people were killed in beautiful Lower Antelope Canyon near Page, Arizona, by a flash flood from a storm that occurred about 15 miles away. In September 2008, a couple died in a canyon flood in Utah, and, in 2005, a group of students drowned under similar circumstances. If caught in a flash flood scramble to higher ground immediately. Also pay attention to potholes full of water. They are normally very slippery and may be deeper than they appear.

PROTECT THE ENVIRONMENT

"The Soil is Alive!" Almost every informational sign in the Moab area and Arches National Park, and the Arches Visitor Guide as well, tells us that desert soil is largely a living entity. Please, be aware of where you are stepping. Biological soil crusts are a very important part of the area's ecosystem. They prevent soil erosion, absorb and hold water, and provide nutrients to plants. One careless footstep can kill hundreds of years of growth.

Crusts are formed slowly by living organisms and their by-products, creating a fragile surface crust of soil particles bound together by organic material. Covering nearly all soil surfaces in the desert, biological soil crust is almost invisible at early stages of growth but over time appears lumpy and black. Help protect fragile crusts by walking on designated trails, bare rock, or streambeds.

The Ten Essentials Systems

The Colorado Mountain Club (CMC), through CMC Press, is the publisher of this pack guide. For more than 100 years, CMC has fostered safety awareness and safe practices in the wilderness, and has distilled the essential safety items to a list known as "The Ten Essentials." We present it here in a "systems" approach. Carrying the items from this list that are appropriate for the location, mileage, and elevation of your hike will help you be fully prepared for every trip and able to survive the unexpected emergency. We encourage all hikers to study, adopt, and teach the Ten Essentials Systems as part of their own outdoors regimen.

1. **Hydration.** Carry at least 2 liters or quarts of water on any hike. For arid country or desert hiking, carry more. Keep an extra water container in your vehicle and hydrate both before and after your hike. Don't wait until you are thirsty—stay hydrated.

2. **Nutrition.** Eat a good breakfast before your hike; pack a full and healthy lunch—including fruits, vegetables, and carbohydrates. Carry healthy snacks such as trail mix and nutrition bars.

3. **Sun protection.** Start with sunscreen with an SFP rating of at least 45 and reapply it as you hike. Wear sunglasses and a wide-brimmed hat, and use lip balm. These protections are important anywhere in Utah, but especially at high elevations and in desert areas.

4. **Insulation.** Be aware that weather in Utah can go through extreme changes in a very short time. Think staying warm and dry—even in arid areas. Dress with wool or synthetic inner and outer layers. Cotton retains moisture and does not insulate well; it should not be

A terrific view of the La Sal Mountains along the Great Pyramid Trail.

part of your hiking gear. Carry a warm hat, gloves, and extra socks. Always include a rain/wind parka and rain pants—on you or in your pack. Extra clothing weighs little and is a great safety component.

5. **Navigation.** You should attain at least minimal proficiency with a map and compass. A GPS unit can add to your ability, but it's not a substitute for the two basics. Before a hike, study your route, and the surrounding country, on a good map of the area. Refer to the map as needed on the trail. This pack guide lists the Trails Illustrated and USGS 7.5 minute maps for the area. Latitude 40 also offers maps of this area.

6. **Illumination.** Include a headlamp or flashlight in your gear, preferably both. With a headlamp, your hands are kept free. Avoid hiking in the dark if at all possible.

7. **First Aid.** Buy or assemble an adequate first-aid kit. Some items to include:

Lower Courthouse Wash rock art site, approximately 2.0 miles south of the entrance to Arches National Park.   PHOTO BY ROD MARTINEZ

- Ace bandages; a bandana, which can double as a sling.
- Duct tape—good for a bandage, blister protection, or rips in your clothes.
- A small bottle of alcohol or hydrogen peroxide for cleaning a wound.
- Latex gloves.
- Specific medications for you and your companions.
- Toilet paper and Ziploc® bags for carrying it out.

Note: This is not a comprehensive list—tailor it and add items for your own perceived needs and intended activities.

8. **Fire.** The best practice is to avoid open fires except in emergency situations. For when you may need to build a fire, carry waterproof matches in a watertight container, a lighter, or a commercial fire starter such as a fire ribbon. Keep these items dry and ensure that all of them will work in cold or wet weather. If needed, tree sap or dry pine needles can help start a fire.

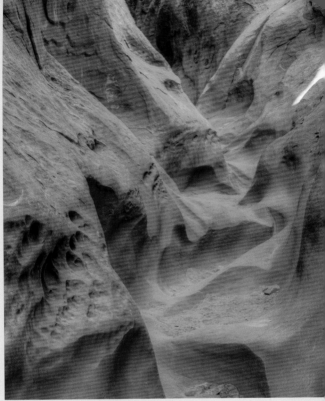

Water sculpts the soft sandstone into pieces of art.

9. **Repair kit and emergency tools.** A pocketknife or multitool and duct tape or electrician's tape are good for various repairs. For emergencies, carry a whistle and signal mirror.

10. **Emergency shelter.** Carry a space blanket and nylon cord or a bivouac sack. Large plastic leaf bags are handy for temporary rain gear, pack covers, or survival shelters. On your way out, use this for trash left by careless hikers.

Photography Tips

We see many beautiful subjects in the outdoors that we would like to remember. Here are a few tips to help you take great photographs and enjoy, time and again, the places where you've been:

- Don't forget to take your camera with you. As you hike, keep it within easy reach.
- Carry extra memory cards so you can take enough photographs to properly record your hike and what you saw.
- Charge your batteries before leaving and take extras if you will be out more than one day.
- Before leaving home, set your camera's resolution to the highest setting possible. Check your manual to see how to do this. Another name for resolution is image quality. You want to use every pixel that you paid for when you bought your camera. A higher setting will give you the ability to capture the light and dark tones as well as all the colors your eyes can see.
- Be prepared. Most hikes start early in the morning, so have your camera out and be prepared to capture the early-morning light on the red rocks or animals moving around.
- Hold your camera steady. The closer the camera is to your face, the steadier it will be. Your photo should not have that unsteady, out-of-focus look.
- Place your whole subject in the frame, and fill the frame with your subject. If you are taking photos of the mountains, be sure to include the tops. Zoom in to crop out those items that do not add to the photo. I recommend vertical photos as opposed to horizontal ones when you are taking photos of trees, flowers, people, and other vertical objects.

The vertical format allows you to increase the size of your subject as you zoom in.

- The best way to learn is from your mistakes. Take lots of photos, trying different angles and settings. Try photographing the same images twice, once with a horizontal orientation and once vertical. Remember, a memory card can be reused, and those pixels are free.
- If all else fails, read the manual.

WILDLIFE VIEWING TIPS

Fade into the woodwork (or woods): Wear natural colors and unscented lotions, if any. Be as quiet as possible—walk softly, move slowly.

Keep to the sidelines: Watch animals from a distance they consider safe. Use binoculars or a telephoto lens to get a closer view. Stay away from nests.

Use your senses
- **Eyes:** Look up, down, and all around for animal or bird signs such as scat, nests, or tracks. Learn to distinguish these wildlife signatures.
- **Ears:** Listen for animal sounds or movement.
- **Nose:** Be alert to musky scents or strange odors.

Think like an animal: When will an animal eat, nap, drink, bathe?

Optimize your watching: The ultimate wildlife-watching experience is of behaviors—viewing animals without interrupting their normal activities. As a rule, dusk and dawn are the best times for this rewarding experience.

—*Rod Martinez*

1. Amphitheater Loop Trail

MAPS	Trails Illustrated, Moab North, Number 500; USGS, Fisher Towers, 7.5 minute
ELEVATION GAIN	283 feet
RATING	Easy–moderate
ROUND-TRIP DISTANCE	3.3 miles
ROUND-TRIP TIME	2–3 hours
NEAREST LANDMARK	Fisher Towers

COMMENT: Utah State Highway 128 from Moab to the historic Dewey Bridge is also known as the Colorado Riverway and/or Scenic Byway 128. It follows the twists and turns of the Colorado River as it carves its way past Professor Valley and eventually into Canyonlands.

On the north side of the highway, red canyon walls rise 900-plus feet above the river, and on the south side of the highway you can glimpse the stately La Sal Mountains, The Priest and Nuns rock spires, and Castle Rock near Castle Valley.

You'll next see the impressive Fisher Towers rising almost 1,000 feet at the far end of Richardson Amphitheater—about 4 miles from the Amphitheater Loop Trail. For a close-up view of Fisher Towers, take the 4.5-mile round-trip trail described in *The Best Grand Junction Hikes,* published by CMC Press.

Richardson Amphitheater was named for Sylvester Richardson, a teacher and postmaster in nearby Professor Valley in the late 1890s. With the help of numerous volunteer groups and under the direction of the Bureau of Land Management, the original trail was constructed in 2004 and an additional 3 miles of loops was added in 2010.

You will probably have the trail to yourself as it does not appear in most older guidebooks, but the solitude is enhanced by a few rabbits, lizards and, in early spring,

Hoodoos along the Amphitheater Loop Trail.   PHOTO BY ROD MARTINEZ

numerous wildflowers. There is no trailhead sign on Highway 128; be aware that the trailhead and information sign are on the north side of Highway 128 by the Hittle Bottom Campground.

GETTING THERE: From the intersection of Utah Highway 128 and US 191, travel east on Hwy 128 for 23.4 miles to the Hittle Bottom Campground.

THE ROUTE: The trail itself begins immediately across Highway 128; use caution in crossing this sometimes-busy highway. The trail is easy to hike, but it is rated as easy–moderate because some effort must be made to follow the trail—it is faint in places and at times the cairns are difficult to locate. After crossing the highway, immediately turn left and hike along the highway for about 75 yards. Then turn right to follow the loop trail in the recommended direction, where you can enjoy views of Castle Rock and Fisher Towers. This stretch of the trail is called the Southern Loop, and it is relatively level.

In 0.5 mile you will descend into a small ravine close to two rather large spires. Follow the cairns until you see a small sign straight ahead. You can take the short trail on the left to a viewpoint and a dead end. Retrace your steps back to the trail. Continue to follow the cairns as you go in and out of a

An impressive cliffed mesa alongside State Highway 128 and Richardson's Amphitheater.

PHOTO BY ROD MARTINEZ

wash for the next 1.0 mile; you will go by another large spire where the wash ends close to a survey post.

The trail then ascends about 300 feet to the top of a ridge. Keep looking for the cairns as you approach the top of the ridge. If you cannot see a cairn, retrace your steps back to the last cairn passed and look ahead. Once on top, continue on the right-hand trail for about 0.5 mile, where it begins to descend at a sign pointing to the Southern Loop or Northern Loop. Take the Northern Loop on your right and continue right for 0.5 mile and look for a large metal survey post with a large cairn to the right of it.

The trail now becomes faint as you enter a wide sandy wash. Look for cairns and wooden posts with arrows to keep you headed in the right direction. About 0.3 mile after the large cairn, you will begin to go under some power lines. Keep them overhead as you continue on the faint trail marked by a few cairns and wooden posts. You will be hiking parallel to Hwy 128; the trail will cross Hwy 128 ending up at the trailhead.

Note: Every hike in this pack guide will end successfully when you are back at your point of origin—the trailhead in most instances. When it is an "out-and-back" hike, we'll advise you to retrace your steps. In the instance of a loop hike, such as this one, follow the directions and stay on trail to get back successfully.

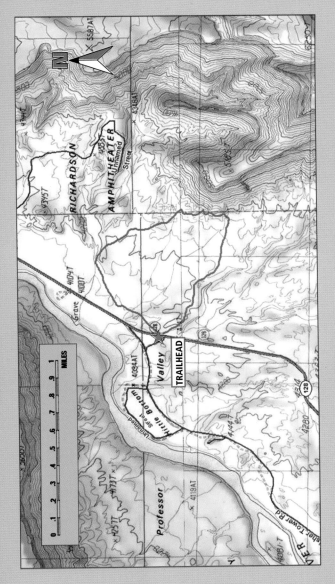

2. Balanced Rock Trail

MAPS	Trails Illustrated, Arches National Park, Number 211; USGS, The Windows Section, 7.5 minute; Arches National Park visitor map
ELEVATION GAIN	Minimal
RATING	Easy
ROUND-TRIP DISTANCE	0.3 mile
ROUND-TRIP TIME	0.25–0.5 hours
NEAREST LANDMARK	Arches National Park Visitor Center

COMMENT: There are probably three or four images that will stay with you from your visit to Arches National Park. One of those memories will likely be of Balanced Rock. The "Rock" is 55 feet high and sits on top of a pedestal that is 73 feet tall.

You will no doubt wonder how the rock maintains its seemingly precarious balance on the pedestal. The answer: The upper rock is composed of an erosion-resistant, slick-rock form of Entrada sandstone. The pedestal is composed of softer Entrada Dewey-type sandstone and is somewhat protected from erosion by the upper portion.

In time the pedestal will erode away from the Balanced Rock and the Balanced Rock will tumble like its renowned neighbor and former balanced rock previously known as "Chip-Off-The-Old-Block." The latter rock fell in the winter of 1975-1976, but the pedestal remains as part of the park's geological history.

As you hike around Balanced Rock, the size of the rock and its estimated weight of 3,577 tons are certain to impress. The views of the Windows Section of the park, as well as the spires and buttes all the way to the 12,000-foot-high La Sal Mountains, are also majestic. As you continue around Balanced Rock, look for different views of the rock and its

Balanced Rock—a 55-foot rock balancing atop a 73-foot pedestal.

PHOTO BY ROD MARTINEZ

balance. The best time of day to photograph Balanced Rock is late afternoon or sunset, when the rock turns a rich red and the sky turns pink and optimizes the appearance of the rock.

GETTING THERE: From the intersection of State Highway 128 and US 191, travel north on Hwy 191 to the park entrance. Take Arches Scenic Drive through Arches National Park for 11.0 miles to the parking area for Balanced Rock.

THE ROUTE: Very often when you arrive at the trailhead the parking lot will be full. Be patient and wait, as cars

Balanced Rock is separate from the surrounding fins and buttes.

PHOTO BY ROD MARTINEZ

drive away from the lot every few minutes. You will be able to avoid most of the crowds if you arrive at sunrise or wait until sunset.

The first 0.2 mile of the trail is concrete, very wide, and wheelchair accessible. There is a very slight elevation gain to the point where the concrete trail ends.

You can return by the same route, but a slightly more primitive trail (not wheelchair accessible) intersects with the concrete trail on your left, about 25 feet before the concrete trail's end. Take the dirt trail for great views of the Windows Section of the park and a long-range view of the La Sal Mountains to the southeast. From this side of Balanced Rock, you get a nice view of North and South Window as well as Turret Arch and the Parade of Elephants, and a hidden view of Double Arch and numerous spires. The view is even more exquisite when the La Sal Mountains are snowcapped, which normally occurs from mid-November to early June.

"Ham Rock" resembles a canned ham—hence its name.

PHOTO BY ROD MARTINEZ

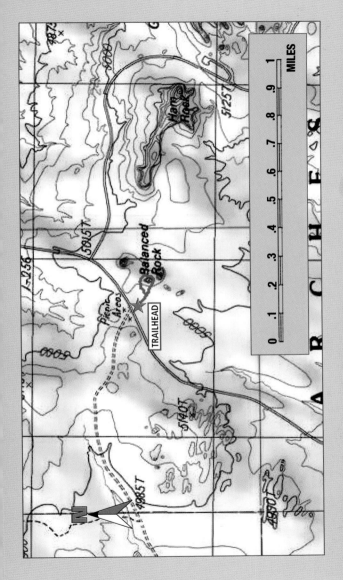

3. Big Horn Overlook Trail

MAPS	Trails Illustrated, Moab South, Number 501; USGS, Shafer Basin, 7.5 minute
ELEVATION GAIN	Minimal
RATING	Easy
ROUND-TRIP DISTANCE	2.5 miles
ROUND-TRIP TIME	1.5 hours
NEAREST LANDMARK	Dead Horse Point State Park Visitor Center

COMMENT: Dead Horse Point State Park consists of about 5,000 acres located on a plateau almost 2,000 feet above a sweeping gooseneck in the Colorado River. The point is located on a peninsula of rock surrounded by sheer sandstone cliffs. The peninsula is connected to the mesa by the Neck, a narrow strip of land only 90 feet wide.

There are numerous stories and legends about how The Point received the name "Dead Horse Point." The most common tale is that, around the turn of the 20th century, some cowboys rounded up a number of wild mustangs and herded them across the narrow neck onto the point. Branches and dead bushes were piled high across the narrow point to form a natural corral; the sheer cliffs denied them any downward escape path. For unknown reasons, as the story goes, the mustangs were abandoned on the waterless point and they eventually died of thirst.

The Colorado River flows 2,000 feet below the visitor center and trailheads. The park is enjoyed by over 200,000 visitors annually. There are over 10 miles of pet-friendly, hiking-only trails. If you bring a pet, please keep it on a leash and clean up after it. Pets are not allowed on the Intrepid System of trails, as it allows both hiking and mountain biking. The Big Horn Overlook Trail will take

Pinnacle resembling the horn of a bighorn sheep on a mesa in Canyonlands.

PHOTO BY ROD MARTINEZ

you to a view of a large but narrow fin of rock that resembles a big set of horns. Due to erosion, the "big horns" look more like horns of a pronghorn antelope than the horns of a bighorn sheep. Across the canyon, you can see Canyonlands National Park, Island in the Sky District.

GETTING THERE: From the intersection of Utah Highway 128 and US 191, travel north on US 191 for 8.6 miles, to where it intersects with Utah Highway 313. Turn left onto Hwy 313 and follow it for 23.3 miles to where the road divides. (The highway on the right goes on to Canyonlands National Park.) Continue straight on Hwy 313 to the Dead Horse Point State Park Visitor Center, 30 miles from your starting point.

THE ROUTE: The trail begins either behind the visitor center or from the campground. (If you are not camping, begin behind the visitor center as there is no additional parking in the campground.) The trail is paved the first 0.3 mile to where it crosses the park road. After crossing the road the trail turns to dirt. In 0.1 mile you will pass by the campground, where there is another sign pointing back to

An old juniper watches over potholes recently filled with rain.

PHOTO BY ROD MARTINEZ

the visitor center, on the right, or the West Rim Trail, on your left.

As you hike to the left, the trail begins to fade in another 0.1 mile. Follow the cairns for almost 0.5 mile to an intersection with the trail to the Big Horn Overlook. Take the trail to the right for 0.9 mile to the Big Horn Overlook.

At times the trail will come close to the edge. Be careful as you take in the panoramic view; look for the cairns on the slickrock that will point the way. After a rain, the potholes fill with water, making an interesting diversion from the normally sandy slickrock trail. At the Big Horn Overlook, the trail ends on a ledge next to a large outcropping on your right. Enjoy the view, the potholes, and the wildflowers, when in season, as you retrace your steps back to the trailhead.

Steep cliffs make for a dramatic view.

PHOTO BY ROD MARTINEZ

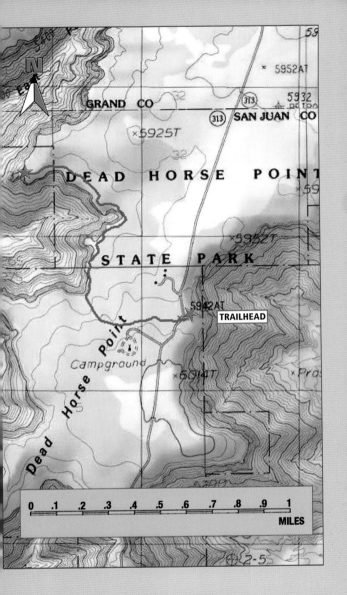

4. Broken and Sand Dune Arch Trail

MAPS	Trails Illustrated, Arches National Park, Number 211; USGS, Mollie Hogans, 7.5 minute; Arches National Park visitor map
ELEVATION GAIN	140 feet
RATING	Easy–moderate
ROUND-TRIP DISTANCE	2.3 miles
ROUND-TRIP TIME	1–1.5 hours
NEAREST LANDMARK	Arches National Park Visitor Center

COMMENT: This is one relatively easy trail to two different and distinct arches. The trail is considered moderate in part due to the need to hike through deep sand.

Sand Dune Arch is only 30 feet wide and 8 feet tall but it sits on top of a very sandy slope that can be a huge sand box for the "kids" in all of us. The arch is in the shade all day long and provides a nice respite from the hot sun. Hike through the deep sand and pass through the arch to the base of the wall, then to a lower bench where you can sit and enjoy your surroundings. The second arch on this trail, Broken Arch, is not actually broken. It appears that way due to a deep notch on the top of the cap rock. Broken Arch is 59 feet high and 43 feet wide and sits on the edge of a slickrock gully.

The views from Sand Dune Arch are limited due to the two encompassing fins that help block the arch. Broken Arch, on the other hand, allows great views; it frames a vista from the 12,000-foot-high La Sal Mountains to the southeast and to the Uncompahgre Plateau on the northeast horizon. Take time to read the Arches Visitor Guide and/or the back side of the Trails Illustrated map, Arches

Broken Arch is not really broken—it is 59 feet high and 43 feet wide.

PHOTO BY ROD MARTINEZ

National Park, Number 211, for good explanations of the geology of the park and how the arches are formed.

GETTING THERE: From the intersection of Utah Highway 128 and US Highway 191, travel north on Hwy 191 for about 2.0 miles to the park entrance. Take Arches Scenic Drive through Arches National Park for 20 miles to the Sand Dune Arch parking area.

THE ROUTE: From the information sign, descend slightly on a sandy trail for 100 yards to an intersection where the short trail on the right leads to Sand Dune Arch and the longer trail on the left leads to Broken Arch.

Follow the trail on your right, which will take you through a very narrow opening through the large fins. The opening is slightly larger than one person wide and the trail becomes very sandy. Trudge slightly uphill through the very deep sand and, about 200 hundred yards from the intersection, turn right and you'll be looking at Sand Dune

Sand Dune Arch resides on a sand dune. The arch is 39 feet wide and 8 feet tall.

PHOTO BY ROD MARTINEZ

Arch. Enjoy the arch and the sand pile before retracing your steps back to the intersection with Broken Arch Trail on your right.

About 0.4 mile from the intersection of the trails to Sand Dune or Broken Arch, you'll come across a trail that can take you to the Devils Garden Campground. Take the right fork, which will take you to Broken Arch, 1.0 mile from the trailhead. As you approach the arch and begin to drop slightly into a slickrock gully, you will see a sign saying "Trail Continues through the Arch." Continuing on this

trail will take you to Devils Garden Campground as well as through the arch. Go through the arch and enjoy the views the arch frames before you retrace your steps back to the trailhead.

Sandstone fins line up like soldiers.

PHOTO BY ROD MARTINEZ

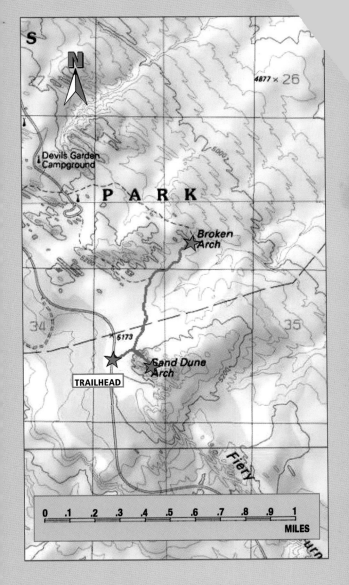

ona Arch Trail

	Trails Illustrated, Moab North, Number 500; USGS, Moab, 7.5 minute
ELEVATION GAIN	440 feet
RATING	Easy–moderate
ROUND-TRIP DISTANCE	3.0 miles
ROUND-TRIP TIME	2 hours
NEAREST LANDMARK	Moab

COMMENT: Although the pathway is designated Corona Arch Trail, your adventure will include two marvelous arches located side by side.

You'll first encounter Bowtie Arch—a natural pothole-formed sandstone arch with a roughly circular opening of about 20 feet. About 600 feet to the left of Pothole Arch is Corona Arch—known as a buttress arch because one end is set in the cliff face.

The opening of Corona Arch is 140 feet wide by 100 feet high—large enough for a small fixed-winged plane to fly through. This, in fact, was accomplished once, but such antics are no longer legal.

Swinging from a rope is still permitted at Corona Arch, but this activity is extremely dangerous, and the Bureau of Land Management is currently considering a ban. The last time I hiked to the arch, a group of four seemingly brave young men were jumping off the top of the arch and then swinging below. I am sure it is a great thrill, but others have been killed trying this stunt.

Corona Arch is nicknamed "Little Rainbow Bridge Arch" as it closely resembles Rainbow Bridge, which is close to Lake Powell near Page, Arizona. Because of its expanse, Corona Arch provides shade almost any time of the year

Corona Arch has an opening 140 feet wide and 100 feet high.

and any time of day. Sit below and gaze upwards at the massive yet elegant curved arch. You can enjoy this arch from either side as there are expansive views from both sides.

GETTING THERE: Travel 1.3 miles north on US Highway 191 to the intersection of Utah Highway 279; turn left and follow Hwy 279 for 10 miles. The parking lot and trailhead for Corona Arch are located on your right.

THE ROUTE: At the information sign, you'll begin a steep ascent. Four sweeping switchbacks take you up the cliff to the first level spot—the trail register box, where you are asked to register. Soon after, you will cross some railroad tracks.

This railroad spur is for the train that runs about weekly from the nearby potash plant to the main line junction at Crescent Junction, near Interstate 70. Take a moment to wonder at the mammoth gorge that was dynamited to create passage for the train.

After crossing the tracks and passing through a turnstile that takes you through the barbed wire fence, follow the abandoned roadbed as it travels through a gap in the canyon rim. As the trail continues to ascend, there are brief respites of level areas. Follow the cairns over a low sandy pass to the base of a large cliff.

Bowtie Arch has a circular opening of 20 feet.   PHOTO BY ROD MARTINEZ

Shortly after the sandy pass—within 100 yards—the trail goes left and you begin hiking on slickrock. When the slickrock becomes a severe slant, there is a safety cable to help keep your feet level. In another 200 yards, there is another safety cable that helps you ascend the "Moki steps" that were chiseled out of the steep slickrock. In about another 50 yards you need to ascend the 10-foot metal ladder taking you to the top of another cliff edge. Once up the ladder, look to your right for your first glimpse of Corona Arch. (You may find its true magnificence lost in the blending of the arch in the cliff face.)

Bowtie is now a few hundred feet straight in front of you and both arches become more impressive as you near them. Follow the cairns for an easy walk on a broad bench that travels beneath Bowtie Arch and Corona Arch. After enjoying the beauty of these arches, retrace your steps back to the trailhead.

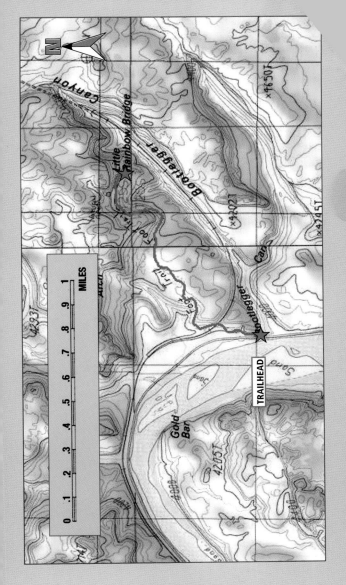

licate Arch Trail

	Trails Illustrated, Arches National Park, Number 211; USGS, Big Bend, 7.5 minute; Arches National Park visitors map
ELEVATION GAIN	480 feet
RATING	Moderate
ROUND-TRIP DISTANCE	3.0 miles
ROUND-TRIP TIME	2.5–3 hours
NEAREST LANDMARK	Arches National Park Visitor Center

COMMENT: Delicate Arch is the iconic image of Arches National Park. After seeing the arch in all its majesty against the backdrop of the La Sal Mountains, you'll understand why its image is the symbol of Utah's Red Rock Country.

Delicate Arch is likely the most photographed arch in Arches National Park. It appears on Utah's license plates, on postcards, and posters—it is the symbol of Utah. Delicate Arch, in comparison to others, is not that large—its span between abutments is 33 feet and it rises to a height of 45 feet above the curved slickrock basin on which it sits. At the proper location, you can photograph the graceful horseshoe shape of Delicate Arch as it frames the La Sal Mountains within its span.

The trail up to Delicate Arch will take you by the site of the Wolfe Ranch Homestead. Built in 1888, this was the only homestead ever established in the area now known as Arches National Park. In 1910 the homestead site was abandoned and, in 1929, 4,520 acres were set aside as a national monument. In 1971, Congress designated Arches as a national park.

Another intriguing site, about 100 yards from the Delicate Arch Trailhead, is a small panel of petroglyphs (see note

Delicate Arch—the iconic symbol of Utah.

PHOTO BY ROD MARTINEZ

below.) The well-preserved panel depicts the life of the Ute Indians and merits a visit on your way to Delicate Arch.

GETTING THERE: From the intersection of Utah State Highway 128 and US 191, travel north on Hwy 191 for about 2.0 miles to the park entrance. Take Arches Scenic Drive through Arches National Park for 14.4 miles. Turn right and travel another 1.2 miles to the trailhead.

THE ROUTE: The trailhead is on the eastern edge of a very large parking lot that is normally full most of the day. From the trailhead, hike past both the side trail to the Wolfe Ranch Homestead and the other trail to the Ute petroglyphs. About 300 yards from the trailhead, you cross over a small bridge. At 0.3 mile from the trailhead, you begin a steep ascent of a small hill, then a gradual descent before another ascent, at 0.4 mile. A little over 0.5 mile from the trailhead, you begin the final steep ascent up the slickrock. The trail now disappears but it is marked by large cairns and the path worn through the upper layers of the slickrock by visitors making their way to Delicate Arch. Stop occasionally,

Petroglyphs on a side trail off of Delicate Arch Trail.

PHOTO BY ROD MARTINEZ

catch your breath, and turn around to see the amazing vistas surrounding you. A little past the 1.0-mile point, the trail has some undulations as you make your way around some large boulders.

At 1.4 miles you reach a ledge that has been carved out of the cliff of a fin of rock that embraces Frame Arch, on your right. The ledge is wide but care must be taken as the edge on the left side falls off about 100 feet.

At 1.5 miles, and around the edge of the fin, Delicate Arch and the massive bowl in front of it are revealed. The walk below the arch is awesome and well worth the hike.

Sit down on the shelf, look at Delicate Arch, and enjoy the splendor before you retrace your footsteps back to the trailhead. Enjoy this extraordinary view, but do not linger too long under the arch as many photographers want to capture that magic image—especially right before sunset. (As an outdoor photographer, I prefer most nature shots with no people in them—especially folks I don't know. So I try to stay out of your photos and hope that you'll return the favor.)

Note: As you roam the West, particularly in Utah, you'll encounter both petroglyphs and pictographs. Petroglyph refers to ancient symbolic art that has been incised, or cut, into the rock surface. Pictographs, also the work of the earliest Native Americans, are paintings on the surface of the rock.

Frame Arch is above the final ledge leading to Delicate Arch.

PHOTO BY ROD MARTINEZ

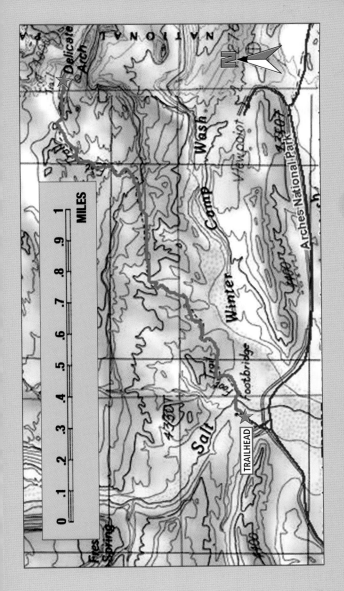

MILES

0 .1 .2 .3 .4 .5 .6 .7 .8 .9 1

N

NATIONAL

Delicate Arch

Arches National Park

Cache Wash

Viewpoint

4340 T

4300 T

4400

4400

Winter

Salt

Trail

Trail

4300

4600

Fres Spring

Footbridge

TRAILHEAD

7. Devils Garden Primitive Trail

MAPS	Trails Illustrated, Arches National Park, Number 211; USGS, Mollie Hogans, 7.5 minute; Arches National Park visitor map
ELEVATION GAIN	343 feet (total elevation change about 1,200 feet)
RATING	Difficult–strenuous
ROUND-TRIP DISTANCE	7.2 miles if all spur trails are hiked
ROUND-TRIP TIME	5 hours
NEAREST LANDMARK	Arches National Park Visitor Center

COMMENT: The Devils Garden Trail can be easy if you hike only to Landscape Arch and back—a distance of approximately 1.6 miles. The trail is difficult to strenuous if you continue past Landscape Arch to Double O Arch, on to Dark Angel Monolith, and return via the primitive loop. If you include the spur trails to Pine Tree and Tunnel Arches, go on to Navajo and Partition Arches, and do the 0.8-mile spur to the 150-foot high Dark Angel Monolith, the total distance is 7.2 miles. The Devils Garden Trail is one of the more popular trails in the Park, with the highlight being the 306-foot wide Landscape Arch.

Landscape Arch is thought by some authorities to be the largest natural rock span in the world; others believe Kolob Arch in Zion National Park is larger. Until a standardized method to measure arches is developed the debate will continue.

After a 73-foot slab fell from the span in 1991, and 47-foot and 30-foot sections fell in June 1995, the National Park Service closed the loop trail beneath Landscape Arch.

As the trail continues past Landscape Arch, you'll ascend a steep slickrock fin—the beginning of the primitive trail to Double O Arch. The upper oval arch of Double O is 71

The impressive Landscape Arch is 306 feet wide.

PHOTO BY ROD MARTINEZ

feet wide by 45 feet high; the lower oval arch is 21 feet wide by 9 feet high.

A 0.8-mile spur trail from Double O Arch leads to the 150-foot tall, desert-varnished spire called Dark Angel. (See desert varnish defined, below.) From this junction, retrace your steps back to the start of the primitive loop trail. This will begin the most difficult and strenuous part of the hike. When following this trail—a little over 2.0 miles back to the main trail by Landscape Arch—pay attention to where the next marker cairn is located. This portion of the trail has some slickrock descents that can be dangerous if you lose your footing. If in doubt about the steepness of the slickrock, resort to descending on your backside. The last 0.5 mile is an ascent on a very sandy trail. After viewing at least eight named arches, you will return to the trailhead, now aware of why this is considered a difficult and strenuous hike.

GETTING THERE: From the intersection of Utah Highway 128 and US 191, travel north on Hwy 191 for about 2.0 miles to the park entrance. Take Arches Scenic Drive through Arches National Park for 20.6 miles to the parking lot for Devils Garden.

Double O Arch—two oval arches together in one sandstone fin.

PHOTO BY ROD MARTINEZ

THE ROUTE: This trail can be done in a variety of lengths and hiking difficulties. As described here, the trail is a difficult and strenuous hike.

The Park Service recommends the primitive loop trail be started 0.1 mile before Landscape Arch and hiked in a counterclockwise direction to return to Landscape Arch. I'll describe the hike in a clockwise direction, as I find it easier to descend the sandy slickrock on my posterior rather than ascending it hand over foot. Whichever direction you take, wear sturdy, cleated hiking boots that can

Navajo Arch—41 feet wide and 13 feet high, an almost perfect semi-circle.   PHOTO BY ROD MARTINEZ

grab the sandstone and help you ascend or descend the steep slickrock.

Be extremely aware of the location of the cairns—they are ranger-placed to ensure you are hiking in the correct direction. This is a wide and hard-packed dirt trail that has some ascents and descents but, overall, has minimal elevation gain.

At 0.25 mile, a 0.4-mile, round-trip spur trail goes to the right to Tunnel and Pine Tree Arches. At 1.0 mile from the trailhead, enjoy the full beauty of Landscape Arch. The primitive part of the trail begins here as you ascend a slick-rock fin for about 100 yards. Here a sign will point to the left; continue about 40 feet past this arrow to a small bush. Work your way down to a lower ledge and, in 25 feet, back to the left and descend down to the trail. At 0.5 mile from Landscape Arch, there is an intersection with a spur trail on the left that will take you 1.0 mile to Partition and Navajo Arches.

After viewing these arches, take the main trail another 0.1 mile to Double O Arch. From Double O Arch the

Pine Tree Arch frames pinon pines.
PHOTO BY ROD MARTINEZ

0.8-mile spur trail will take you to Dark Angel. As you traverse to and from Dark Angel, enjoy the view of the Klondike Bluffs to the west and the impressive Fin Canyon to the east.

Upon returning from Dark Angel, go left onto the primitive loop trail. This will take you back to Landscape Arch in 2.1 miles. Always be aware of the cairns as you travel 0.4 mile to another spur trail that will take you to Private Arch. This is a secluded arch that is worth the extra 0.4-mile hike. (This is not included in the 7.2-mile stated length for the entire Primitive Loop Trail.)

After retracing your steps back to the main trail, you will begin descending the steep slickrock and sandy fins. Continue to be aware of the location of the cairns, especially on top of and down from the fins. The last 0.5 mile back to Landscape Arch is a steady, sandy ascent. Stop, rest as needed, and drink plenty of water. Upon reaching the wide Landscape Arch Trail, retrace your steps back to the trailhead.

Note: Throughout this pack guide, we have included arch measurements consistent with what the National Park Service uses on their website, visitor center brochure, and signs. The science of measuring arches continues to improve; many sources now list Landscape Arch as 290.1 feet wide and 77.5 feet high. Regardless of its exact width, you'll be sure to marvel at this natural wonder!

Desert varnish

Desert varnish is aptly named—it is Mother Nature painting her Western rock faces in colors ranging from deep red to black. Although it may appear to derive from water coursing down vertical rock surfaces, desert varnish is much more a product of wind-borne microorganisms attaching to rock faces over the millennia.

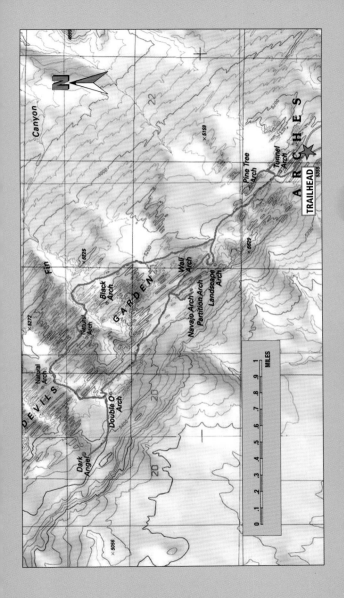

8. Goblin Valley-Carmel Canyon Trail

MAPS	Trails Illustrated, San Rafael Swell, Number 712; USGS, Goblin Valley, 7.5 minute; Goblin Valley State Park brochure
ELEVATION GAIN	Minimal
RATING	Easy
ROUND-TRIP DISTANCE	1.5 miles
ROUND-TRIP TIME	1–2 hours
NEAREST LANDMARK	Hanksville, Utah

COMMENT: Goblin Valley State Park is another jewel in Utah's lineup of beautiful state parks. The 3,654-acre park was dedicated in 1964.

Because of the soft sandstone, the formations are eroded into a multitude of different shapes. With no two alike, interesting photography, as well as exploration and fun for the kids, is readily available. A surreal appearance is created by the grotesque shapes and shadows early in the morning and late in the afternoon.

Galaxy Quest, the parody science fiction film, was filmed at Goblin Valley in order to depict unearthly scenery.

Goblin Valley State Park is relatively small—about 1.0 mile wide by 2.0 miles long—but it contains thousands of mushroom-shaped pinnacles, or hoodoos, of different heights. These formations have large orange-brown boulders sitting on top of the weaker sandy layers. These bottom layers continue to erode more quickly from rain and wind than the harder boulders resting on top of them. Besides the "normal" goblins, you will walk by, or through, tall hoodoos, flat-topped goblins, short caves, small arches, and horizontal hoodoos. The only variance in the red-brown color of Goblin Valley is an occasional green bush.

Just a few of the thousands of "goblins" in Goblin Valley State Park.

PHOTO BY ROD MARTINEZ

There are a few marked trails in the park, but most visitors spend an hour or two just wandering around the goblins. Maps and a brochure of the area are available at the visitor center.

Whether you wander or try to follow a trail, keep the observation point in view as a constant reminder of your location. The San Rafael Desert is to the east of Goblin Valley; the San Rafael Swell is located to the west. There are a number of slot canyons (please read the side note on them) located in the San Rafael Swell. Little Wild Horse Canyon, as described on page 74 of this pack guide, is one of the most picturesque slot canyons in the area.

In October 2013 two Boy Scout leaders purposely toppled one of the rock formations. Serious charges were filed and the leaders were dismissed from the Boy Scouts. Help maintain nature by staying on the trails and leave all formations, rock art, etc. as you found them.

GETTING THERE: From the intersection of Utah Highway 128 and US 191, travel north 29 miles to Interstate 70. Turn left (west) onto I-70. At 61.8 miles, exit I-70 (at Exit 149) and turn left onto State Highway 24. At 86.2 miles, turn right onto Temple Mountain Road. At 93.4 miles, turn left onto Goblin Valley State Park Road. The entrance to Goblin Valley State Park is at 98.3 miles. Turn left and the entrance station is at 102.7 miles. Continue on the entrance road and, at 103.6 miles, turn left. The observation point and trailhead is at 104.3 miles.

THE ROUTE: While you could wander about and around the rock formations, to maintain the physical integrity of the park it is best to follow designated marked trails. The three trails are:

Curtis Bench—an easy 2.1-mile round-trip trail that will give you a unique overview of the valley as well as terrific views of the Henry Mountains.

Entrada Canyon—a moderate 2.6-mile round-trip trail from the campground to the goblins and back.

Carmel Canyon—if you can only hike one trail, this is the one to do. This easy trail will take you from the parking lot and observation point to the desert floor. Descend the wooden platform steps and you can begin to explore the goblins on the desert floor. There are no cairns or specific trails to lead you through the myriad of goblins. Stay in those areas where there is hard-packed sand and it is evident where others have walked. The trail, as such, will take you to many different areas around the desert floor.

Please respect the goblins and balanced rocks by only taking pictures. Do not try to push the balanced rocks off their pedestals, or sit or climb on the goblins. It has taken eons to create these goblins. Enjoy their uniqueness and let nature continue to erode them at her own pace. After an hour or more of fun, look for the picnic area/observation point and retrace your steps back to the trailhead.

Hoodoos and pinnacles

The National Park Service definition of a hoodoo: "Hoodoos are tall skinny spires of rock that protrude from the bottom of arid basins and 'broken' lands. In common usage, the difference between hoodoos and pinnacles, or spires, is that hoodoos have a variable thickness often described as having a 'totem pole-shaped body.' A spire, on the other hand, has a smoother profile or uniform thickness that tapers from the ground upward."

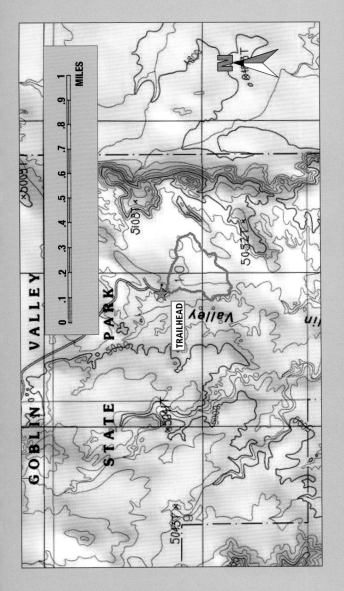

9. Great Pyramid Loop Trail

MAPS	Trails Illustrated, Moab South, Number 501; USGS, Shafer Basin, 7.5 minute
ELEVATION GAIN	Minimal
RATING	Moderate
ROUND-TRIP DISTANCE	4.2 miles
ROUND-TRIP TIME	2 hours
NEAREST LANDMARK	Dead Horse Point State Park Visitor Center

COMMENT: Dead Horse Point State Park is divided into two areas, one strictly for hiking and one for both mountain biking and hiking.

The Great Pyramid Loop Trail is part of the Intrepid Loop System of mountain biking trails. Because the Webster Dictionary defines intrepid as "feeling no fear or very bold or brave," hikers may feel this trail is not meant for them. In fact, the trail is so named because of a generous contribution to the park from the Intrepid Potash Company.

The three mountain biking trails of the Intrepid Trail System are: Intrepid Loop—1.1 miles; Great Pyramid Loop—4.2 miles; and Big Chief Loop—9.0 miles. The Intrepid and Great Pyramid Loop trails provide great hiking.

The Big Chief Loop is not recommended to hikers by the state park rangers because of its length and distance from the visitor center.

The Great Pyramid Loop is a moderate hike of 4.2 miles that will take you to two scenic overlooks—The Colorado River Overlook and the Pyramid Canyon Overlook.

The Intrepid Trail System was built as a set of mountain bike trails in 2009 by a group of volunteer organizations. The Great Pyramid Loop Trail is easy to follow; the path is beaten by mountain bikers and the cairns are well placed.

A mesa resembling the Great Pyramid in Egypt.   PHOTO BY ROD MARTINEZ

I thought I might encounter a number of mountain bikers on the trail, but only saw four, and a couple of other hikers, during the two hours I spent on the trail. The trail has minimal elevation gain, some sandy washes, and slickrock sections, but, more important, incredible scenery. The destination is an overlook into Pyramid Basin and Pyramid Butte that has a strong resemblance to the Great Pyramid in Egypt. The Colorado Overlook is a grand overlook to the Colorado River, which winds its way past the Intrepid Potash Mine evaporation ponds 2,000 feet below.

GETTING THERE: From the intersection of Utah Highway 128 and US 191, travel north on US 191 for 8.6 miles, to where it intersects with Utah Highway 313. Turn left onto Utah 313 and follow it for 23.3 miles to where the road divides. (The highway on the right goes to Canyonlands National Park.) Continue straight on Utah 313 to the Dead Horse Point State Park Visitor Center, 30 miles from your starting point.

THE ROUTE: The Intrepid Trail System begins by the visitor center, on the north end of the parking lot. The hiking and biking trails run together for the first 100 yards. A sign points to the hiker-only trail on the right. In about 200

A juniper guards the cliff edge on the Great Pyramid Trail.

yards ascend some slickrock to a sign indicating Pyramid Canyon Loop at 4.0 miles, and Pyramid Canyon Overlook at 1.5 miles.

Two hundred yards from this sign another sign will point you to the Colorado River Overlook, just a few yards away. Retrace your steps back to the main trail. The hiking and biking trails are now combined to form one easy trail to follow.

The trail has some elevation gains and losses, but they are hardly noticeable as you enjoy the view of the La Sal Mountains and canyons. At 1.9 miles from the trailhead, a sign will point you to the Great Pyramid Overlook. Enjoy the view into the deep canyon and then to the bluff that closely resembles the Great Pyramid.

Retrace your steps back to the main trail, where a sign will point you to the visitor center on the left, or to the right to the group camping site. Go to the right and, in about 100 yards, the trail will make a sweeping curve around and to the top of a ledge with a terrific panoramic view.

On the ledge, a sign will point to the right for The Big Chief Loop. Another sign will point you back to the Pyramid, but a smaller sign with a map also has the Pyramid on it. Go to the left of the smaller sign. After 0.6 mile, this trail combines with the Raven Roll bike trail. After 1.2 miles, the trail rejoins the Intrepid Trail. Continue straight for 0.3 mile to the trailhead and visitor center.

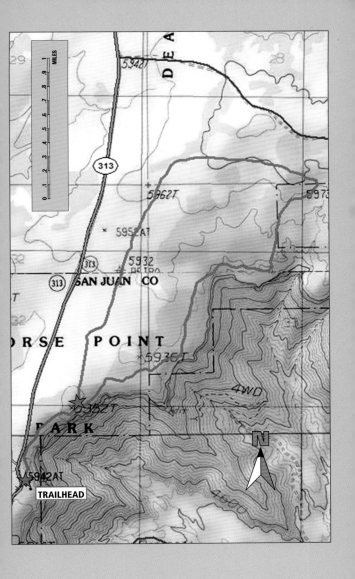

10. Hidden Valley Trail

MAPS	Trails Illustrated, Moab South, Number 501; USGS, Moab, 7.5 minute
ELEVATION GAIN	680 feet
RATING	Moderate
ROUND-TRIP DISTANCE	5.3 miles
ROUND-TRIP TIME	4 hours
NEAREST LANDMARK	Moab

COMMENT: This is one of the easier trailheads to locate in the Moab area. This is a great trail for a quick day hike; you can return to Moab by lunch. It is also used by locals to get some great exercise all year round. Despite how close it is to town, it does not seem to be heavily used. This trail is also used as part of a loop of the Moab Rim biking trail. It is not one of the favorites for mountain bikers in the area because of boulders, large rocks, and a tough ascent/descent. Even though the trail goes through a wilderness study area, the route is bike-legal.

On your ascent and descent, you will get some very nice views of the Moab Valley. Once on top of the ledge and at the end of Hidden Valley, terrific views of the Behind the Rocks area unfold before you. The trail continues until it intersects with the Moab Rim four-wheel-drive road. It is recommended you turn around at the top of the pass. This will save you a descent that would need to be ascended to return to the trailhead. Continuing the extra 0.33 mile to the road will make the total length of the hike 6.0 miles.

Hidden Valley is green and lush during the early spring or after a number of soaking rains. The view to the La Sal Mountains is especially impressive with a full coat of snow in the winter or early spring months.

Hidden Valley Trail bisects the valley between the Moab Rim and Spanish Valley.

GETTING THERE: From the intersection of Utah Highway 128 and US 191, travel south for 6.3 miles and turn right on Angel Rock Road. At 6.7 miles turn right onto Rim Rock Lane. The road becomes dirt at 6.9 miles and the trailhead is at 7.0 miles—at the end of the road.

THE ROUTE: The trail begins with a slight ascension on the left side of the information sign. The trail goes up even more as you approach the trail registration box. Please sign in at the registration box and sign out after you complete the hike.

The trail ascends a series of steep switchbacks for about the next 0.8 mile. As you go up you will be sidestepping some large boulders and large rocks. There are a few cairns to lead you up the trail. The switchbacks consist partially of scree that will be slick on your descent.

The trail levels out as you enter Hidden Valley. Hidden Valley is a shelf between the top of the Moab Rim and Spanish Valley. It received its name because it is hidden from the Moab Valley floor. As you follow the trail into Hidden Valley, look down to the valley floor to see how far you have ascended in a relatively short distance. After a short distance into Hidden Valley, you will notice and remark

Slickrock makes for a formidable barrier on the left side of the valley.

how quiet it has become—the surrounding fins and cliffs block the sound of the vehicles below. The trail continues relatively level as it goes over a low rise that separates the two halves of Hidden Valley. From the low rise it is approximately 1.0 mile to a low pass. Here you have a great view of the large sandstone fins of the Behind the Rocks area. The trail continues for another 0.33 mile to the Moab Rim four-wheel drive road. Retrace your steps back to the trailhead.

The Moab Rim rises above the Hidden Valley floor.

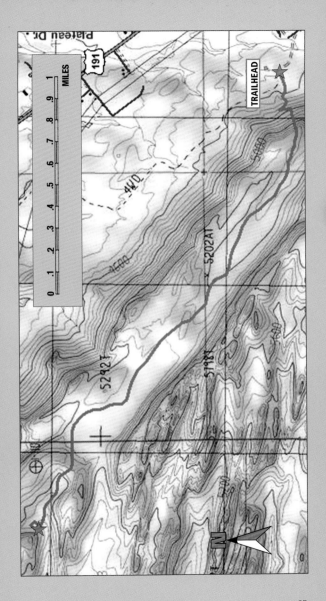

11. Horseshoe Canyon Trail

MAPS	Trails Illustrated, Maze District, Number 312; USGS, Sugarloaf Butte, 7.5 minute
ELEVATION GAIN	780 feet
RATING	Difficult–strenuous
ROUND-TRIP DISTANCE	6.5 miles
ROUND-TRIP TIME	5–6 hours
NEAREST LANDMARK	Green River, Utah

COMMENT: Horseshoe Canyon is part of the Maze District of Canyonlands National Park. The 3,200 acres comprising Horseshoe Canyon were added to the Park in 1971 in an attempt to protect and preserve the rock art along the length of the canyon. There are four distinct panels of pictographs and petroglyphs located in Horseshoe Canyon.

The rock art found in Horseshoe Canyon is painted in a style known as "Barrier Canyon." Barrier Canyon rock art has been dated from 2,000 B.C. to 500 A.D. The Great Gallery is the best known and most well preserved site.

The Great Gallery panel is approximately 200 feet long and 15 feet high. There are 20 life-sized, anthropomorphic figures in the panel. One of these figures is over 7 feet tall. The figures have a ghostly appearance, are lacking appendages, and have tapered bodies. The largest figure, known as the Holy Ghost, has large, hollow eyes in a skull-like head. This is one rock art panel you won't forget.

There are three other major panels in the canyon. The first is High Gallery, so named because of its location high up on the canyon wall. The Living Site, or Horseshoe Shelter—the second site—contains more ghost-like figures than the High Gallery panel. The Alcove Site—the third panel—has been vandalized, with most of the panel destroyed. These panels have been preserved for thousands

The Great Gallery Panel is approximately 200 feet long by 15 feet high.

of years; please continue to help preserve them. Something as slight as touching them or tracing them in chalk hastens their deterioration. The rock art panels are the main reason to drive to and hike Horseshoe Canyon.

An added attraction is some dinosaur tracks located on the trail. Two of them are found approximately 100 yards before you reach an old watering trough. The three-toed tracks are about 12 inches in length. The best and easiest to see track is about a foot off the main trail. It is highlighted by layers of rock encircling the track. Once again, observe and only take photos.

Horseshoe Canyon itself is worthy of a hike to view the high sandstone walls. Wildflowers and mature cottonwood groves along the intermittent stream enhance your hike in the canyon. Carry binoculars or a telephoto lens to view the rock art from a safe distance.

GETTING THERE: From the intersection of Utah Highway 128 and US 191, travel north for 29 miles to Interstate 70. Reset your odometer at this intersection. Turn left onto I-70 and travel west 17.4 miles to Exit 164. Exit I-70 and turn right on County Road 19. At 20.5 miles, turn left onto Long Street. At 20.9 miles turn left onto a short piece of unnamed roadway; at 21.0 miles, turn right onto Airport Road. At 21.4 miles you will go under I-70. At 23.2 miles and a Bureau of Land Management (BLM) sign, turn left to Horseshoe Canyon. The road now becomes hard-packed dirt. At 50.6 miles, another BLM sign points straight ahead to Horseshoe Canyon. At mile 51.8, continue straight. At 63.6 miles,

"The Holy Ghost" is the largest figure in the Great Gallery.

PHOTO BY ROD MARTINEZ

turn left at the third BLM sign to the trailhead. At 65.4 miles you will arrive at the trailhead and an information sign.

THE ROUTE: The trail begins to descend directly behind the information sign. The trail is well marked and distinct as you descend by an old water tower located on your left. Be aware of the mentioned dinosaur tracks located adjacent to the main trail. In another 0.5 mile you will go through a fenced barricade as you continue to descend.

The next 0.25 mile, and final descent to Barrier Creek in Water Canyon, is through deep sand. In ascending the 780 feet back to the trailhead, this deep sand will test your leg muscles.

After reaching the creek, take a right turn and hike by the large cottonwood trees. In 0.5 mile, look high and to the left on the east canyon wall to view the High Gallery panel of rock art. The second panel, known as either Living Site or Horseshoe Panel, is almost directly across the wash from the High Gallery on the west canyon wall. Continue down the canyon for a few hundred yards where the third panel, Alcove Site, is located on the west canyon wall. Over time, natural and human activity have damaged the pictographs. Continue to follow cairns downstream for 1.25 miles to the Great Gallery and enjoy the magnificence of this world-renowned art site.

Take advantage of the shade created by the cottonwoods before you retrace your steps and then ascend through 780 feet of deep sand back to the trailhead. Take your time. This is one more time when you will be glad you have carried plenty of water.

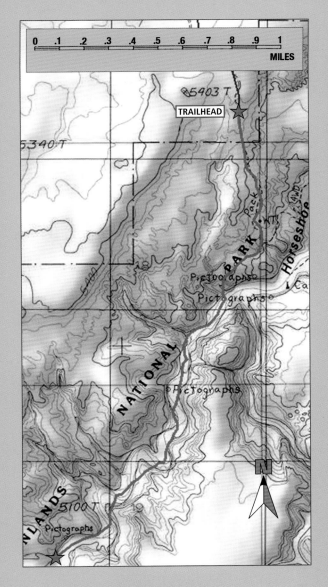

12. Hunter Canyon Trail

MAPS	Trails Illustrated, Moab South, Number 501; USGS, Moab, 7.5 minute
ELEVATION GAIN	Minimal
RATING	Easy
ROUND-TRIP DISTANCE	4 miles
ROUND-TRIP TIME	2 hours
NEAREST LANDMARK	Moab

COMMENT: Hunter Canyon is one of the few red rock canyons that contain water long enough during the year to give the hiker stately cottonwoods for shade at any time.

The canyon is also lush with tamarisk, willows, and, at times, poison ivy. The stream that winds through Hunter Canyon is fed by a spring that may not be flowing in late winter and early spring. When it is flowing, the hike through the canyon is more interesting, as the trail crosses the stream several times. This can make the trail harder to follow due to washouts created by summer flooding from thunderstorms.

If you lose the trail, back up and try again—the canyon is rather narrow and the trail does not meander far from the stream. The trail passes between high red rock cliffs and is sandy with some intermingling of slickrock all the way to the turnaround point.

During early spring, the canyon is full of wildflowers and large clumps of prickly pear cactus. The canyon becomes very colorful when the prickly pear are in full bloom during late spring.

About 0.5 mile from the trailhead, there is a rather large arch high on the cliff face, on the right-hand side. The arch blends in with the canyon wall, but as you approach

Hunter Canyon Arch—approximately 74 feet high.   PHOTO BY ROD MARTINEZ

a rather large rock in the trail, look up for the arch. As you hike another 100 feet past the large rock, the span of Hunter Arch is now at its best exposure. When you travel to Hunter Canyon along Kane Creek Road, be aware of numerous panels of rock art, with the most photogenic being the famous Birthing Scene. The Birthing Scene is a large rock with petroglyphs on all four sides. The most distinct petroglyph is a woman with her arms and legs outstretched giving birth. Look for the feet extending from the birthing sac.

GETTING THERE: From the intersection of Utah Highway 128 and US 191, travel south into Moab. After 3.1 miles, turn right onto Kane Creek Boulevard. In 0.8 mile, you'll intersect with 500 West; continue straight for another 3.9 miles—7.8 miles from the intersection—where the pavement ends. In another 2.0 miles, you'll drive down some steep switchbacks and, after another 1.0 mile, you will arrive at the Hunter Canyon Trailhead.

THE ROUTE: The trail starts at the information sign, but there are numerous side trails to a few primitive camping spots. From the large cottonwood at the trailhead, stay in the sandy wash for about 100 yards, where you will cross the stream for the first time. In another 100 yards, you will cross back over the creek as the trail works its way around some more large cottonwoods.

In 50 yards more, you'll find a wooden sign pointing to the trail. You will continue to cross the creek several times, and more wooden posts point the way. At 0.25 mile from the trailhead you will see the trail register; please take the time to sign in.

At 0.5 mile from the trailhead, you will encounter a large rock in the middle of the trail. You can skirt around it on the left to cross back over the creek or walk through the large opening in the rock, then cross the creek and find the trail on the left side.

Be sure to look up high on the cliff on the right side for a great view of Hunter Arch. The trail remains fairly level, but there is a fork in it after another 100 yards; stay to the right by the large cottonwood. In a few yards you will see a large cairn on the right. Cross the creek again and scramble through some tamarisk to find the trail. You'll now continue on the left side and, 1.0 mile from the trailhead, if the stream is flowing you will see the first of a few small waterfalls and numerous pools of water. As you continue up Hunter Canyon, look up at the large pinnacles on your right and marvel at the desert varnish as it paints the red canyon walls.

At 2.0 miles there is a large alcove on the left and the brush

becomes thicker as you cross the stream another time. You can fight through the brush for a while longer before turning back, or turn around now and retrace your steps to the trailhead.

The creek through Hunter Canyon creates picturesque waterfalls.

PHOTO BY ROD MARTINEZ

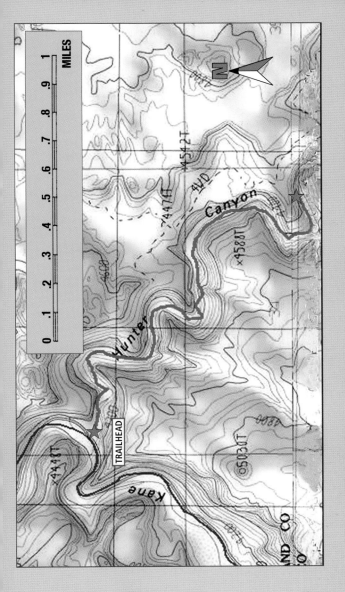

13. Little Wild Horse Canyon Trail

MAPS	Trails Illustrated, San Rafael Swell, Number 712; USGS, Little Wild Horse Mesa, 7.5 minute
ELEVATION GAIN	500–600 feet
RATING	Moderate
ROUND-TRIP DISTANCE	6 miles
ROUND-TRIP TIME	3–4 hours
NEAREST LANDMARK	Hanksville, Utah

COMMENT: The San Rafael Swell is a large geologic feature located about 30 miles west of Green River, Utah. It is about 75 miles long by 40 miles wide. The Swell is a giant, dome-shaped anticline of sandstone, shale, and limestone which was pushed up or raised 40 to 60 million years ago. (See note on anticlines, below.) Flash floods have eroded the sedimentary rock into valleys, gorges, mesas, buttes, and slot canyons—like Little Wild Horse Canyon located in the southern part of the Swell.

The area is managed by the BLM. While the Swell does not currently enjoy any special protection, parts of it are being considered for protection as wilderness areas.

The San Rafael Swell attracts hikers, backpackers, horseback riders, and ATV enthusiasts. The Swell is also home to a number of rock art sites and at least 12,000 dinosaur bones.

One of the more popular areas in the Swell is Little Wild Horse Canyon. The walls of this canyon are very high and there are very tight narrows from top to bottom as the canyon twists and turns. The canyon is also flush with different colors and textures that can be a photographer's delight, especially in the early morning or late afternoon.

The water-carved Navajo narrows of Little Wild Horse Canyon wind through the rock for a mile or more. You may have to squeeze and twist your way through the rock in parts of the canyon that are only 3 to 6 feet wide. Also, there are some rock obstacles where you may need to go up, over, or around.

In places, only one person at a time can ascend or descend the narrow canyon. It periodically opens to wider spots where you can witness the true beauty of the entire canyon. After a rainstorm or snowmelt higher up, there will be potholes full of water that will require some wading and the trail may be very muddy and slick underfoot.

The trail into Little Wild Horse Canyon narrows to as little as three feet. PHOTO BY ROD MARTINEZ

Always be aware of impending weather. Thunderstorms can create flash floods, which are extremely dangerous and can pose a great risk to people hiking in narrow canyons. (Please read the safety note on water and canyons on page 17.)

You can do this loop hike in conjunction with Bell Canyon. The loop hike with Bell Canyon is 8 miles in length. Doing the loop hike will require some routefinding skills in order to locate Bell Canyon. Hike into the canyon only as far as you feel comfortable. I recommend hiking a little more than 3 miles. At this point the canyon widens, trees and bushes become dominant, the narrows disappear, and you will begin an ascent to the connecting dirt road to Bell Canyon.

GETTING THERE: From the intersection of Utah Highway 128 and US 191 in Moab, travel north on Hwy 191 29 miles to Interstate 70. Turn left (west) onto I-70. At 61.8 miles, exit I-70 (at Exit 149) and turn left onto Hwy 24. At 86.2 miles,

You will need to duck to get under this large boulder.

PHOTO BY ROD MARTINEZ

turn right onto Temple Mountain Road. At 93.4 miles, turn left onto Goblin Valley State Park Road. The entrance to Goblin Valley State park is at 98.3 miles. Turn right here; the trailhead is on your right at 98.8 miles.

THE ROUTE: The hardest part getting into and up Little Wild Horse Canyon is a few hundred yards from the trailhead. The trail begins to the right of the restrooms. Stay on the bank for about 50 yards—a sign will direct you into the wash. After about 200 yards there is a 6- to 8-foot-high dry waterfall. Ascending this waterfall requires some good scrambling skills or a boost up from behind. A better alternative is to watch for a small sign and faint trail to the left. This bypass ascends a ledge, allowing you to circumvent the dry waterfall. This ledge, however, is narrow and precarious. Your descent, in about 100 yards, is steep and rocky, so be cautious.

Once off the ledge, the trail separates in about 200 yards. The trail to the left ascends into Bell Canyon. Take the trail on the right to begin the hike into Little Wild Horse Canyon. In another 100 yards or less, you will begin to enjoy the narrows and the real beauty of Little Wild Horse Canyon. The total length of the narrows is a little over a mile. Continue to where the canyon opens up and widens and the narrows end. Retrace your steps and enjoy the beauty of Little Wild Horse Canyon from a different perspective as you descend back to the trailhead.

Anticlines and synclines

An *anticline* is a geologic structure formed by rock strata being compressed, forced upward, and then folding down on the sides. (Think of the letter "A.") A *syncline*, which often occurs in conjunction with an anticline, is the trough that results at the bottom of a geologic fold. (Think of the lower part of the letter "S.)

14. Mill Creek Canyon Trail

MAPS	Trails Illustrated, Moab South, Number 501; USGS, Moab, 7.5 minute
ELEVATION GAIN	Minimal
RATING	Easy
ROUND-TRIP DISTANCE	1.5 miles
ROUND-TRIP TIME	1–1.5 hours
NEAREST LANDMARK	Moab

COMMENT: Moab is the hub of Red Rock Country. US Highway 191 divides the City of Moab as well as the numerous hikes in the area. Places to explore on the west side of US 191 are Canyonlands National Park, Dead Horse Point State Park, Goblin Valley State Park, and Horseshoe Canyon. Other hikes on the west include, but are not limited to, trails up Potash Road and Kane Creek, all located within just a few miles of downtown Moab.

Areas to hike and explore on the east side of US 191 are Arches National Park and the Colorado Riverway—including Negro Bill Canyon and the Fisher Towers area. Also on the east side are some lesser known areas: Sand Flats Recreation Area, Ken's Lake, and, one of my favorite hikes, Mill Creek Canyon.

Mill Creek is a sparkling stream lined with lush vegetation. Another feature of Mill Creek Canyon is the ancient rock art scattered along the canyon walls. Because of the lush vegetation, however, it is usually hard to find.

One hundred years ago Mill Creek helped generate electricity for the Moab Valley. The first dam on the creek was made of wood; it was destroyed in the flood of 1919. What was left of the wooden dam was replaced with a concrete dam later that year. The use of Powerhouse Dam was discontinued in 1945 when a large power line was built, stretching from Price, Utah, to Moab.

Mill Creek originates about 20 miles southeast of Moab, in the heart of the La Sal Mountains. This trail ends at a large pool of water at the base of a set of beautiful waterfalls. Some people dive from the top of these waterfalls into the pool of water. I don't recommend doing this as the pool is relatively shallow and the water may not absorb the shock of an errant dive.

Dramatic waterfalls on Mill Creek at the Powerhouse Dam.   PHOTO BY ROD MARTINEZ

There are a number of pools to wade in, located at the base of the waterfalls by Powerhouse Dam. Once again, these are not diving pools. To reach these pools, take the trail immediately on your left at the parking lot. Mill Creek Trail is encumbered only by a large number of dogs and hikers. There is a trail to the right of the parking lot that goes up onto a ledge. This is a hiking and biking trail, but it is used more by mountain bikers than hikers.

GETTING THERE: From the intersection of Utah Highway 128 and US 191, travel 2.8 miles south on US 191 and turn left onto 300 South; at 3.2 miles, turn right onto 400 East. At 3.3 miles, turn left onto Mill Creek Drive. At 3.8 miles, turn right as you continue on Mill Creek Drive. At 4.3 miles, turn left onto Powerhouse Lane. At 4.5 miles, the pavement ends, and at 4.9 miles, you will arrive at the parking lot and trailhead.

THE ROUTE: The trailhead is located behind the information sign. Walk west for about 100 yards to the Powerhouse

Mill Creek winds its way downcanyon to Moab.

PHOTO BY ROD MARTINEZ

Dam, then walk around the right side of the building to continue on the main trail.

You'll arrive at a rock ledge about 75 yards from the metal sign for bike parking. The rocks are very sandy and slick, so be very careful going across this short ledge. It is best to immediately drop down into Mill Creek. Continue to follow the trail along the creek. At times you may need to stoop to get under the vegetation and walk or wade through Mill Creek. Wear sandals or shoes that will allow you to comfortably wade in the water. Have fun and be refreshed on a hot day.

At a little over 0.25 mile the trail divides. The hard-to-discern trail on the right goes up Mill Creek. The more dominant trail on the left takes you up the North Mill Creek fork. Stay left at the fork to reach the waterfalls and the large pool.

From the pool it is difficult to hike or climb to the top of the waterfalls as the falls and surrounding rock are slick. If you want to hike to the top of the waterfalls and slide down into the pool, you will need to backtrack on the trail. In order to do this, retrace your steps towards the trailhead for about 300 yards. Look for a side trail on your right. Hike and scramble up the ledge to a faint trail that will lead you to the top of the waterfalls. If you want to take a longer hike, this trail does continue further up the North Fork of Mill Creek Canyon. Otherwise, have fun in the water before retracing your steps back to the trailhead. You could hike this trail every afternoon, just to be refreshed.

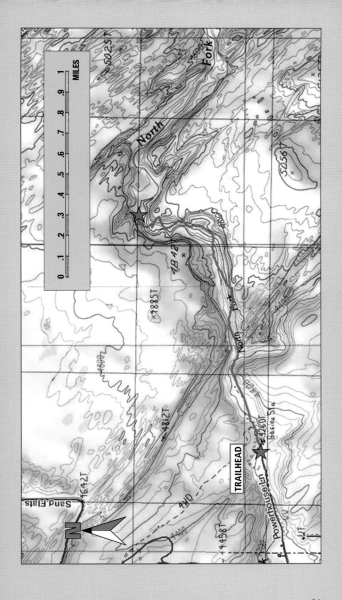

15. Negro Bill Canyon Trail

MAPS	Trails Illustrated, Moab North, Number 500; USGS, Moab, 7.5 minute
ELEVATION GAIN	330 feet
RATING	Easy–moderate
ROUND-TRIP DISTANCE	4.5 miles
ROUND-TRIP TIME	3–3.5 hours
NEAREST LANDMARK	Moab

COMMENT: When I first hiked this trail, about 15 years ago, the parking lot was small, had a dirt surface, and there were few people around. Now you'll find the parking lot large, paved, and full of cars.

The trail follows a perennial stream that you will have to cross 10 times. Rocks are placed in the streambed in many places, so rock-hopping will keep your feet dry, especially if you have a long stride. Sandals or waterproofed boots can be a big asset.

There is poison ivy at spots along the stream but especially at the end, where the pool forms in front of Morning Glory Natural Bridge. Look at the information sign at the trailhead to learn what poison ivy looks like. It can be very bothersome if you interact with its leaves.

There is some rock scrambling required as you follow the trail. Due to the stream, the canyon bottom is lush and green and numerous small trees offer shade. At times a side trail may lead you astray for a few yards; just back up and follow the main trail.

As you hike the canyon, look at the red canyon walls that, in places, are painted in "desert varnish." In Negro Bill Canyon, desert varnish is black because it is composed of

Morning Glory Natural Bridge—the world's sixth largest natural bridge.

a large amount of manganese and iron, but Mother Nature has delicately painted it in a variety of patterns. Negro Bill Canyon is a large and beautiful Navajo Sandstone gorge that will take you to 243-foot-long Morning Glory Natural Bridge—the sixth-largest natural rock span in America. After the bridge, you can continue up the canyon for a number of miles, but it becomes rugged and harder to follow. The first non-Caucasian pioneer in the Moab area was William Granstaff. He was a successful rancher in the area that now bears his name in a more colorful way.

GETTING THERE: From the intersection of Utah Highway 128 and US 191, follow Hwy 128 east for 3.1 miles to the trailhead located on the south side of the highway.

THE ROUTE: The trail begins on the left bank of the stream. The first part of the trail is remarkably level and, after 0.25 mile, you will be in a wilderness study area. After 0.4 mile,

Desert varnish paints the red canyon walls of Negro Bill Canyon.

PHOTO BY ROD MARTINEZ

the trail widens but continues along the side of the stream. At 0.75 mile, the trail makes a short ascent and then levels off again.

After about 1.0 mile, you will make your first of 10 stream crossings. A side canyon leads to the right after the fifth stream crossing, but stay to your left on the main trail as you continue the stream crossings on your way to Morning Glory Natural Bridge. After the last stream crossing, at 2.0 miles from the trailhead, the trail veers to the right again as you ascend the last 100 yards to your destination.

Be sure to avoid the poison ivy around the pool of water in front of Morning Glory Natural Bridge. Look for the stream of water that can be seen and heard as it flows directly out of a fracture in the rock face. Enjoy the water as you retrace your steps back to the trailhead.

The perennial stream nourishes the lush vegetation in Negro Bill Canyon.

PHOTO BY ROD MARTINEZ

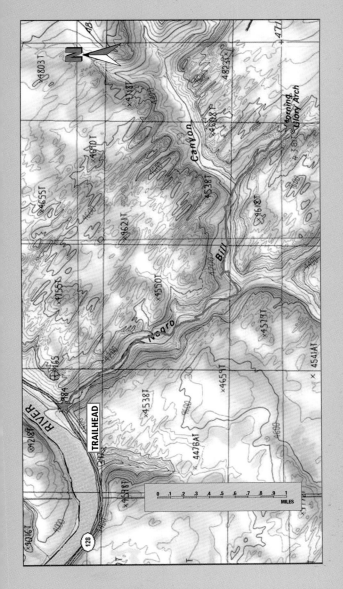

16. Park Avenue Trail

MAPS	Trails Illustrated, Arches National Park, Number 211; USGS, The Windows Section, 7.5 minute; Arches National Park visitor map
ELEVATION GAIN	320 feet
RATING	Easy–moderate
ROUND-TRIP DISTANCE	2.0 miles
ROUND-TRIP TIME	1 hour
NEAREST LANDMARK	Arches National Park Visitor Center

COMMENT: Park Avenue Trail takes you through a canyon of sheer red rock towers. You will feel like you are walking down a broad city avenue with tall skyscrapers on both sides. The first 100 yards of trail—from the trailhead to the overlook—is made of concrete and is wheelchair accessible. From the overlook, you can see Courthouse Towers, Sausage Rock (look closely to see the resemblance to a sausage), and Queen Nefertiti Rock on your left. The latter rock bears a resemblance to the ancient Egyptian queen and is balanced atop a spire—you'll wonder how it maintains its balance.

Farther ahead and on your left is Sheep Rock. The Tower of Babel is straight ahead at the end of Park Avenue. Organ Rock is slightly to the south of the Tower of Babel. Again to your left are the Three Gossips who appear to be "gossiping" about the many tourists who hike this trail.

As you leave the overlook and descend into the dry canyon wash, continue to observe the tall spires. It is speculated that some of them are the abutments of ancient arches that collapsed over the eons. If you wish to make this an easy hike, you can arrange for a car shuttle to meet you at the Courthouse Towers viewpoint. For a more moderate hike, retrace your steps and ascend the 320 feet in elevation as you walk back to the trailhead.

Queen Nefertiti Rock balances on top of a spire alongside Park Avenue.

GETTING THERE: From the intersection of Utah Highway 128 and US 191, travel north on Hwy 191 for about 2.0 miles to the park entrance. Drive through the park on the only paved road, Arches Scenic Drive, for 5.1 miles. The trailhead is on the left.

THE ROUTE: The trailhead begins to the right of the information sign. At the overlook, begin your descent into the dry wash leading to the canyon bottom. For the first 0.33 mile, the descent is down 111 stone steps. At times these are not evenly spaced, but they do allow a safer trip to the bottom.

As you leave the steps, follow the cairns as they lead you through the dry wash. This trail is easy to follow as you walk along the canyon bottom because the area is not very wide and chances of getting off trail are minimal. Remember, the rangers built the cairns to help guide you on the trail in the direction you need to go to have a safe and fun hike. Building your own cairns, or knocking down the ranger-built cairns, may lead a fellow hiker to go in the wrong direction.

From the trailhead you have an unimpeded view through Park Avenue.

You will make a slight ascent as you approach Arches Scenic Drive. If you did not arrange for a car shuttle, begin retracing your steps back and up to the trailhead. I rate this

trail as tending to moderate, rather than just easy, because you have to navigate the 111 stone steps and 320-foot ascent. Continue to admire the rock spires on your way back for another perspective on how they resemble their names. This is a great hike to do earlier in the morning to avoid the crowds and the bright sun of midday.

The Tower of Babel is the turnaround point for Park Avenue.

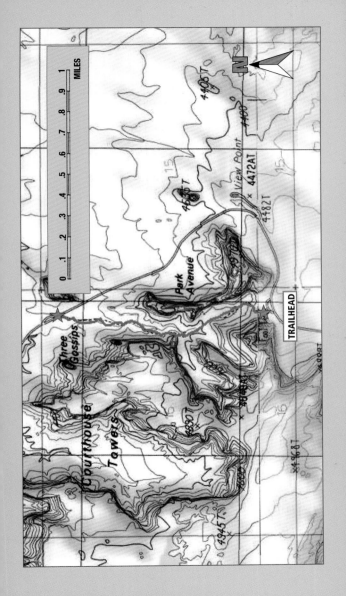

17. Portal Overlook Trail

MAPS	Trails Illustrated, Moab South, Number 501; USGS, Moab, 7.5 minute
ELEVATION GAIN	980 feet
RATING	Moderate–difficult
ROUND-TRIP DISTANCE	4 miles
ROUND-TRIP TIME	3 hours
NEAREST LANDMARK	Moab

COMMENT: The Portal Overlook Trail will take you to a precarious ledge and superb panoramic views, showing 360 degrees of the Colorado River, Arches National Park, the La Sal Mountains, and the Moab Valley.

The length of the trail is in question: a BLM sign at the trailhead indicates it is 1.5 miles to the overlook. At the trail register box, (0.5 mile up the trail), however, the information sheet inside the box says the trail to the overlook is 2.0 miles. After hiking the trail and using the Moab topo map and a GPS, I believe the trail is 4 miles round-trip from the trailhead.

This trail is popular with citizens of Moab because it is close to town and can provide a great leg workout. The trail is also popular with mountain bikers as it provides access to Poison Spider Mesa.

Normally, mountain bikers go down the trail in order to make a loop ride from the Poison Spider Mesa Trailhead. It takes some skill to descend this trail on foot; it is an even more demanding challenge for expert mountain bikers. Hikers should be aware of descending mountain bikers and concede the right of way on the trail.

The ascent to the overlook via the trail is a little less than 1,000 feet in a little more than a mile. This creates a difficult

A view of Moab Valley from the Portal Overlook Trail.

ascent and an equally tough descent going back to the trailhead. The trail is comprised of switchbacks, narrow dangerous ledges, a good deal of loose rocks, and steep steps. Once you reach the end of the trail on the ledge at the viewpoint, be extremely careful as one false step could result in a fall of several hundred feet off the edge. Wildflowers in the spring are abundant, the views are terrific, and the workout is arduous—all on a trail very close to Moab.

GETTING THERE: From the intersection of US 191 and Utah Highway 128, travel north on US 191 for 1.5 miles. At the intersection with Utah Highway 279, turn left and travel 4.2 miles to the Jaycee Park Recreation Site, on your right. The trailhead is located on the east end of the small parking lot by the information sign.

THE ROUTE: The trail is level for the first 0.5 mile as it travels through a shady stand of willows and scrub oak alongside Utah Highway 279. The prickly pear cactus and their delicate flowers help line the trail for 0.5 mile to the trail register box, where the trail begins its ascent to the overlook. Please take a minute to register.

As you begin to ascend the very rocky trail, look behind you and enjoy the view of the Colorado River beginning its journey into Canyonlands National Park. The numer-

The Colorado River winds below and past the Portal Overlook Trail.

ous switchbacks help ease the burden of elevation being gained as you ascend the slickrock ramps of sandstone to the overlook. Be mindful of the cairns as the trail will seem to disappear on the slickrock.

After about 2.0 miles, and an elevation gain of 980 feet, you will arrive at the observation point and the end of your hike. The trail does continue on to the top of the mesa but it becomes increasingly precarious and I recommend that most hikers not try to go on. Turn around and descend the steep and rocky trail back to the trailhead.

A multitude of sandstone fins stand between the Portal Overlook and the La Sal Mountains.

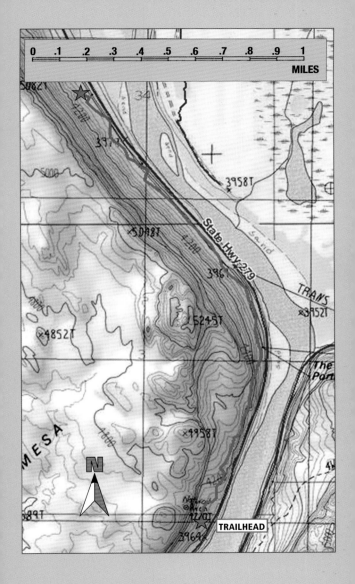

0 .1 .2 .3 .4 .5 .6 .7 .8 .9 1
MILES

State Hwy 279

TRAILHEAD

MESA

N

18. Rim Loop Trail

MAPS	Trails Illustrated, Moab South, Number 501; USGS, Shafer Basin, 7.5 minute
ELEVATION GAIN	Minimal
RATING	Moderate
ROUND-TRIP DISTANCE	5.4 miles
ROUND-TRIP TIME	4 hours
NEAREST LANDMARK	Dead Horse Point State Park Visitor Center

COMMENT: Most visitors would agree that Dead Horse Point State Park is one of Utah's truly spectacular parks. It is located between the better-known Arches National Park and Canyonlands National Park, Island in the Sky District. The beauty of this park and its location close to Moab more than compensate for its smaller size—a few square miles, or approximately 5,000 acres.

Many years ago, officials of San Juan County, Utah, believed this part of the state to be scenically spectacular. They purchased 628 acres from the Bureau of Land Management and donated the land to the State of Utah for a state park. In 1959, five years before Canyonlands National Park was designated a national park, Dead Horse Point was dedicated a state park.

The Rim Trail begins behind the visitor center and traverses the west side of the rim of the park. It then joins the paved trail to and around the Dead Horse Point portion of the trail. After hiking this portion the trail, continue along the east rim back to the visitor center. As you hike the trail, take time to walk the spur trails to see parts of the canyon you would miss by just staying on the main trail. The Rim Overlook is a 0.5-mile round-trip trail, and will give you nice views of the canyon rim on the west side of Dead Horse Point State Park.

The gooseneck of the Colorado River as seen from Dead Horse Point.
PHOTO BY ROD MARTINEZ

The Shafer Canyon Overlook spur trail, also a 0.5-mile round-trip trail, provides a terrific view into Shafer Canyon and the Shafer Trail. The Shafer Trail is a very steep four-wheel-drive road that drops down to the White Rim Road. This combination is a difficult and technically demanding 100-mile road, from the rim of Canyonlands National Park.

Meander Overlook is a short but worthwhile spur trail that provides great views of the Colorado River as it meanders through the canyons 2,000 feet below.

Dead Horse Point Overlook has an almost 360-degree panoramic view of the state park, Canyonlands, and the La Sal Mountains. The best time of day to photograph this magnificent scene is at sunset, when the canyons are bathed in varying colors of yellow, orange, and red. The Basin Overlook, another 0.5-mile round-trip spur, provides a view of the bright blue evaporative ponds of the Intrepid Potash Mine. The view to Pyramid Butte, Chimney Rock, and ending at the La Sal Mountains, makes this short spur trail also worthwhile.

GETTING THERE: From the intersection of Utah Highway 128 and US 191, travel north on US 191 for 8.6 miles, where it intersects with Utah State Highway 313. Turn left onto Hwy 313 and follow it for 23.3 miles to where the road divides—with the highway on the right going on to Canyonlands National

Park. Continue straight on Hwy 313 to the Dead Horse Point State Park Visitor Center, 30 miles from your starting point.

THE ROUTE: The Rim Trail is a combination of the East Rim and West Rim Trails. The trail begins behind the visitor center or from the campground. (If you are not camping, begin behind the visitor center as there is no additional parking in the campground.) The trail is paved the first 0.3 mile to where it crosses the park road. After crossing the road, the trail turns to dirt.

In 0.1 mile, you will pass by the campground, where there is another sign pointing back to the visitor center, on the right, or the West Rim Trail, to your left, to continue your hike. The trail begins to fade in another 0.1 mile, but follow the cairns for almost 0.5 mile to an intersection with the trail to the Big Horn Overlook.

Continue straight for 0.2 mile to the Rim Overlook Trail. After hiking to the rim, retrace your steps back to the main trail and continue 0.5 mile to the Shafer Canyon Overlook spur trail. Retrace your steps back to the main trail yet one more time, and continue on your right for 0.5 mile to the short spur trail to Meander Overlook.

After retracing your steps to the main trail again, continue 200 yards to The Neck parking lot. Follow the paved path around The Point, where after another 0.5 mile the trail continues as the dirt East Rim Trail. After 0.5 mile, the

Basin Overlook spur trail— 0.5 mile round-trip—will be on your right. Retrace your steps back to the main trail and the 0.6-mile finish to the visitor center.

The Colorado River from the Meander Overlook at Dead Horse Point State Park.
PHOTO BY ROD MARTINEZ

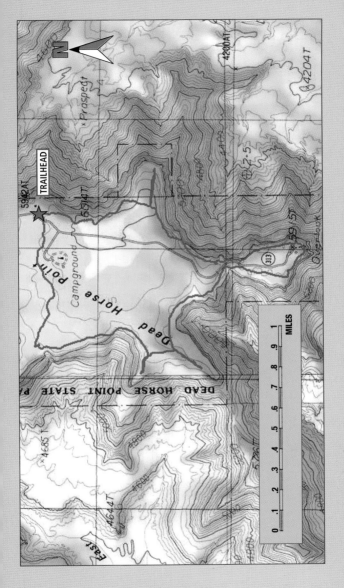

19. Tower Arch Trail

MAPS	Trails Illustrated, Arches National Park, Number 211; USGS, Klondike Bluffs, 7.5 minute; Arches National Park visitor map
ELEVATION GAIN	100 feet
RATING	Difficult
ROUND-TRIP DISTANCE	3.4 miles
ROUND-TRIP TIME	3 hours
NEAREST LANDMARK	Arches National Park Visitor Center

COMMENT: If you want a diversion from the crowds enjoying so much of Arches National Park, this is the trail for you. Tower Arch Trail will lead you to a large oval arch, 101 feet wide by 45 feet high, lying beneath a very large and tall sandstone tower—hence the name Tower Arch.

Getting to the arch from the main park road could be a challenge. The road is very "washboardy" and travel at a speed more than 15 MPH may shake loose body and automobile parts. There is also a portion of the road that is very sandy as it travels through a wash.

Check with the park rangers to see if there has been any rain or snow in the area in the last couple of days. Avoid the road if rain is impending. Be aware that the road may be closed at any time. All that being said, the road can still be traveled by almost any passenger vehicle.

Klondike Bluffs, where Tower Arch is found, is located in the far northwest corner of the park. Because of its remoteness, and the difficult road, Tower Arch has few visitors in comparison to the rest of the park.

The parking area at the trailhead is small; please be aware of how and where you park so emergency and official vehicles can have access if needed. As you hike to Tower Arch, you will pass an eroding sandstone fin that has left

Tower Arch, 101 feet wide and 45 feet high, stretches below a large
sandstone tower.   PHOTO BY ROD MARTINEZ

tall thin towers that strongly resemble marching men or
soldiers standing at attention. Parallel Arch is located on
the right side of the trail, a little over 100 yards before you
reach Tower Arch. This arch is easier to see as you leave
Tower Arch and retrace your steps back to the trailhead.

GETTING THERE: From the intersection of Utah Highway 128
and US 191, travel north on Hwy 191 for about 2.0 miles
to the park entrance. Take Arches Scenic Drive through
Arches National Park for 19.3 miles and take a left on the
dirt road. A gate will indicate if the road is open or not.
(You might want to inquire first at the visitor center.)
Travel 7.2 miles on the sandy washboard road to where it
intersects with the four-wheel-drive road. Continue past
there for about 0.1 mile and take the second left turn onto
Tower Arch Trailhead Road. Drive an additional 1.0 mile to
the small parking area and trailhead.

THE ROUTE: Tower Arch Trail is located immediately beside
the information sign. The trail is level for the first 50 to 75
feet, then begins a steep ascent for 200 yards to the top of
the mesa.

The Marching Men spires along the Tower Arch Trail.

PHOTO BY ROD MARTINEZ

Once you are on top, the trail is level until 0.5 mile from the trailhead. It then begins to descend on a gentle to moderate grade. Be aware of the cairns and follow them—this trail is not heavily used and can disappear if rain or wind obliterates prior footprints.

About 0.8 mile from the trailhead, the Marching Men towers appear on your left and you can also enjoy a great view of the La Sal Mountains to the southeast. The trail crosses two sandy dry washes before making a steep ascent through very deep sand to another level area by an arrow sign.

In another 200 yards, you will descend on sandstone fins and Parallel Arch will appear on your right. Continue right and work your way through a narrow slot between two fins, where you will be at the base of Tower Arch and the large spire behind it.

Take the time to scramble up the slickrock base to enjoy a break under the large arch and the shade it provides. If you have time, search for and scramble to another view of the arch and surrounding spires. Retrace your steps back to the trailhead. As you descend the last 200 yards to your vehicle, be cautious of your steps down this very steep slickrock.

Note: After finishing this hike, you may wonder about its "difficult" designation. Two things were factored into this: First is the short but steep, possibly slippery, portion of the trail that you will encounter almost right away—and on your return. Second, there are two portions of the trail where it is necessary to trudge through deep sand. Our philosophy is to err on the side of caution in setting the degrees of difficulty attached to each trail description.

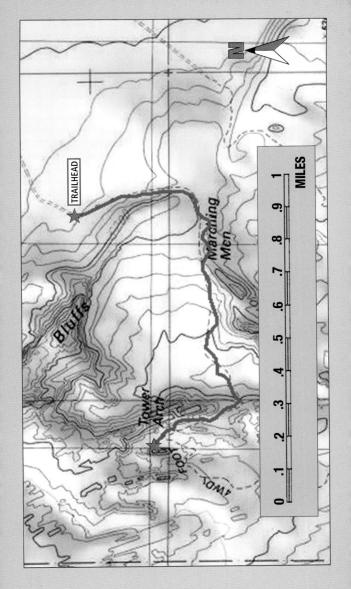

N

TRAILHEAD

Marching Men

Bluffs

Tower
Arch

FOOT

4WD

MILES

0 .1 .2 .3 .4 .5 .6 .7 .8 .9 1

20. The Windows Section Trails

MAPS	Trails Illustrated, Arches National Park, Number 211; USGS, The Windows Section, 7.5 minute; Arches National Park visitors map
RATING	Easy
ROUND-TRIP DISTANCE	1.1 miles
ROUND-TRIP TIME	1 hour
NEAREST LANDMARK	Arches National Park Visitor Center

COMMENT: The trails in the Windows Section provide a great place to spend time casually visiting a number of arches and rock spires that resemble elephants. All of the trails in the Windows Section are rated easy.

The South Window is 56 feet high and 115 feet wide; the North Window is 51 feet high and 93 feet wide. Turret Arch actually has three arches in its large fin—the largest arch is 64 feet high and 39 feet wide, the second largest is 13 feet high and 12 feet wide, and the smallest is 8 feet high by 4.5 feet wide.

As described below, Double Arch is a distinct arch and the short trail to it is about 0.25 mile north of the Windows Trail, at a separate trailhead. The trail to Double Arch is not described here, but it is worth the effort to see this second-largest natural rock opening in Arches National Park. The larger eastern span is 160 feet between abutments and rises 105 feet above the ground. The smaller, western arch is 60 feet wide and 61 feet high and opens into the "Cove of Caves." The opening between these two arches is also considered a separate, and third, arch.

South of Double Arch is a distinct rock formation, The Parade of Elephants, that resembles a herd of elephants marching while holding each other's tails.

The North and South Windows in Arches National Park.

GETTING THERE: From the intersection of Utah Highway 128 and US 191, travel north on Hwy 191 for about 2.0 miles to the park entrance. Take Arches Scenic Drive through Arches National Park for 11.9 miles and turn right onto the unnamed road to the Windows Section. After 2.5 miles the trailhead and a very large parking area will be on the right side of the road. Park here for the trailhead to the Windows Arches, or continue another 0.25 mile to the trailhead and the large parking area for Double Arch. If desired, you can park in either parking lot and walk to the other trailhead.

THE ROUTE: The trails are easy and wide as you leave the parking area. The hard-packed gravel trail heads southeast for 0.1 mile to where it intersects with a trail that will intersect with another trail after another 0.1 mile. Take the right fork at both intersections—up to the distinct fin that houses Turret Arch. After going under the arch, continue following the wide path to the intersection of the Windows Trail. At this intersection the trail to the left will take you to North Window and the trail to the right will take you to South Window, where it ends at a large scenic overlook.

Retrace your steps back down to the trail, where it will go by South Window and intersect with the primitive trail and loop you back to the parking lot. The primitive trail is not as wide as the Windows Trail but it will give you a

Turret Arch—a fin with two arches.

different look at both the South and North Windows. Follow the cairns and stay on the trail. If you want to hike up and into the Windows arches, there are side trails that will take you up to them, but some rock scrambling will be

required. Continue on the primitive trail and make a small ascent up a hill, around the edge of the fin, and back to the main trail and parking area. (Visiting Double Arch requires walking or driving 0.25 mile to the Double Arch Trailhead. The trail is not described here, but the short hike is well worth the time and effort.)

The impressive Double Arch is on its own trail in the Windows Section.

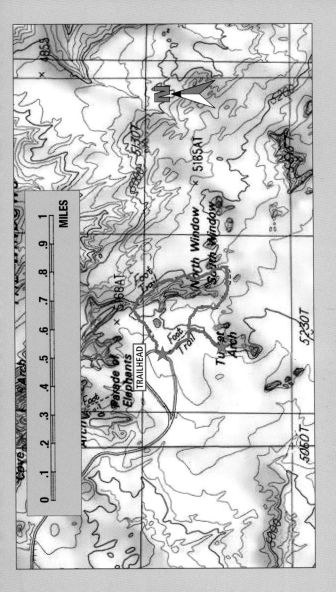

About the Author

Rod Martinez has always loved spending time outside. As a kid growing up in Cripple Creek, Colorado, he explored the nearby hills and old mines. As he grew older, he found another love—photography. In time he discovered 35mm photography and a lifelong passion was born. Rod has climbed 17 of Colorado's Fourteeners and has hiked in almost all of the western states, primarily in Colorado, Utah, and northern Arizona. He has combined his two passions to visually capture nature's beauty on every hike. Rod's work has resulted in him being named Grand Junction's Photographer of the Year for four years in a row. In 2001, he helped form the Southwest Photographic Arts Association Camera Club, and he currently teaches photography and leads photo workshops. Rod joined the Colorado Mountain Club in 2000 and has served as program director, treasurer, and trail steward for the Western Slope Group. Rod has authored *The Best Grand Junction Hikes*, *The Best Telluride Hikes*, and *The Best Aspen Hikes* pack guides. Rod has also written a few articles for *Trail & Timberline*, CMC's quarterly magazine, and has had his photographs published on the cover of *Trail & Timberline*.

A different view of the unbroken Broken Arch.

PHOTO BY ROD MARTINEZ

Checklist

THE BEST MOAB AND ARCHES NATIONAL PARK HIKES

Get Outside.

Become a CMC Member, today!

Explore the mountains and meet new people with the Colorado Mountain Club. Join us for trips, hikes, and activities throughout the state! Join today and save with special membership promotions for our readers: www.cmc.org/readerspecials

The Colorado Mountain Club is the state's leading organization dedicated to adventure, recreation, conservation, and education. Founded in 1912, the CMC acts as a gateway to the mountains for novices and experts alike, offering an array of year-round activities, events, and schools centered on outdoor recreation.

When you join the Colorado Mountain Club, you receive a variety of member benefits including:

- 20% member discount on CMC Press books
- 15% member discount on CMC hats, t-shirts, and hoodies
- 40% off admission to the American Mountaineering Museum
- Discounts at various outdoor retailers
- 4 issues of *Trail & Timberline* magazine
- FREE signups to over 3,000 mountain adventures annually
- Access to courses, classes, and seminars throughout the state
- Adventure Travel opportunities to take you to the world's great destinations